CLINT EASTWOOD

CLINT EASTWOOD

ROBERT TANITCH

STUDIO
VISTA

FOR PETER AND ELIZABETH CORNISH

Studio Vista
an imprint of Cassell
Wellington House, 125 Strand
London WC2R 0BB

British Library Cataloguing in Publication Data
A catalogue record for this book is available from the British
Library

ISBN 0-289-80132-X
First published 1995

Distributed in the United States by
Sterling Publishing Co. Inc.
387 Park Avenue South, New York, NY 10016-8810

Distributed in Australia by
Capricorn Link (Australia) Pty Ltd
2/13 Carrington Road
Castle Hill, NSW 2154

Typeset by Litho Link Ltd, Welshpool, Powys, Wales
Printed and bound in Great Britain by Bath Press Limited

Frontispiece: Clint Eastwood in *High Plains Drifter*

Also by Robert Tanitch

A Pictorial Companion to Shakespeare's Plays

Ralph Richardson, A Tribute

Olivier

Leonard Rossiter

Ashcroft

Gielgud

Dirk Bogarde

Guinness

Sean Connery

John Mills

Brando

Contents

Introduction

Clint Eastwood, one of the great film stars and icons of the twentieth century, has been at the top of his profession for over 30 years. This book is a pictorial record of his career from the 1950s to the present day.

Clint Eastwood, actor, director and producer, has always had an instinct for what the public wants and he has achieved popularity across a wide range of genres: Western, detective, thriller and comedy. Though, initially and regularly, accused of being wooden, technically weak and having only one expression, he quickly established himself with the cinemagoing public. The critics, seemingly immune to his personality, humour and sex appeal, tended to underestimate him, both as an actor and as a director, and they did so precisely because he was so successful.

Eastwood, tall, lean and laconic, an actor of strong physical presence and loose-limbed grace, has been likened to a gazelle in jeans and cowboy boots. Totally confident in his masculinity and totally without vanity, he has always been able to mock his macho image; indeed, so often has he taken his image apart that it has seemed at times as if he wanted actively to erode it altogether.

He is famous for having created two charismatic cult heroes, The Man With No Name and Dirty Harry, two superguns, ultra cool, solitary, single-minded characters, deceptively lethargic, with hidden reserves beneath their stoical exterior.

Eastwood knows his limitations as an actor and within those limitations he has climbed mountains, scaled a fortress, escaped from prison, driven a bus through a hail of bullets, driven a steam train into a saloon bar, flown over the Arctic in a supersonic fighter and been chased by a dinky car all over San Francisco.

In his films, he has run a travelling Wild West Show, served in Korea, Vietnam and Grenada, gone AWOL to rob a bank behind enemy lines and saved the life of the President of the United States of America.

His roles have found him auditioning for the Grand Ole Opry at Nashville, falling in love with a country and western singer, having an affair with a murderess, making friends with an orang-utan, developing a taste for bondage, being picked up by a gay in Madison Gardens and talking to the trees (but they didn't listen to him). He has also been lynched, raped, castrated and come back from the dead on more than one occasion . . .

Clint Eastwood was born in San Francisco on 31 May 1930 and educated at Oakland Technical High School and Los Angeles City College. Before he became an actor he did a number of jobs, including lumberjack, steel-furnace stoker, gas-station attendant and swimming instructor, the latter while he was in the army from 1950 to 1954.

His film career, which began in 1955 with bit parts in a number of instantly forgettable films, took off four years later when he landed the second lead in a new television Western series, *Rawhide*, which proved so popular that it lasted until 1966. (It has been revived constantly ever since.) The Italian director Sergio Leone saw him in episode 91 (*The Incident of the Black Sheep*) and, having failed to get an American star with a bigger name, offered him the leading role in *Per un pugno di dollari* (*A Fistful of Dollars*, 1964), which was so phenomenally successful in Italy (outgrossing *My Fair Lady* and *Mary Poppins*) that they went on to make two sequels, *Per qualche dollari in più* (*For a Few Dollars More*, 1965) and *Il buono, il brutto, il cattivo* (*The Good, the Bad and the Ugly*, 1966).

Audiences expecting such old-fashioned things as romanticism, morality, honour and loyalty (the traditional ingredients of a Hollywood Western) were in for a violent awakening. The critics hated it. 'Everyone susceptible to the illusion that shooting and killing with fancy flourishes are fun can indulge his bloodlust to the fullest,' wrote the *New York Times*. The public loved it. The Man With No Name became a cult figure on a par with James Bond and Eastwood's career was completely transformed. Vittorio de Sica declared he was the new Gary Cooper and cast him in the fifth episode of *Le Streghe* (*The Witches*, 1966), an indifferent portmanteau vehicle for his wife, Silvana Mangano, which has rarely been seen outside Italy.

His first starring role in an American Western was in *Hang 'Em High* (1968), which explored the pros and cons of capital punishment. It was not long before he was being hailed as John Wayne's heir, though his anti-heroes were as far removed from Wayne's screen persona as can be imagined. *Coogan's Bluff* (1968), a sharp, off-beat thriller, which followed, began a long and profitable association with Don Siegel. Coogan established Eastwood as the maverick in action and can now be seen, with hindsight, as a dummy run for Dirty Harry.

Brian Hutton directed him and Richard Burton in Alastair MacLean's *Where Eagles Dare* (1968), an incredibly silly World War II adventure, which was dismissed as

Clint Eastwood in Two Mules for Sister Sara

'dreadful piffle', 'corny cliffhanger', 'unashamed hokum', 'turgid tosh', 'two-fisted idiocy', 'a mindless bloodbath', and went on to become 1969's biggest earner.

He played the juvenile lead in Alan Jay Lerner and Frederick Loewe's *Paint Your Wagon* (1969), opposite Lee Marvin, the first and last time he would appear in a musical, though not the last time he would sing on screen. So appalled was he by the waste of money on location that he decided to form his own production company, Malpaso (named after a creek near his home in the Carmel area), which gave him the opportunity to produce, direct and star in his own productions in a more economical manner.

He starred with Shirley MacLaine in *Two Mules for Sister Sara* (1969), an enjoyable, tongue-in-cheek, comedy-romantic adventure, which he has described as 'African Queen Goes West'. *Kelly's Heroes* (1970), a large-scale spoof of wartime heroics, a blockbusting mixture of mordant humour, crude slapstick and loud explosives, proved equally popular. 'Men,' said Brian Hutton, its director, 'like to see Eastwood in action. Women like to see him in anything.'

Don Siegel always believed *The Beguiled* (1970) to be his best film. Unfortunately, the producers, keen to get Eastwood's fans to see it, made the error of giving what was essentially an art-house movie a commercial release, with the result that the movie flopped at the box office. His regular audience didn't like the idea of him being castrated and poisoned and stayed away in large numbers. Eastwood has been quoted as saying that *Beguiled* would probably have been more successful if he hadn't been in it.

Sixteen years before *Fatal Attraction*, there was a first-rate adult thriller called *Play Misty for Me* (1971), which marked his debut as a director and was also notable for a brilliant and frightening portrait of sexual paranoia by Jessica Walter.

Dirty Harry (1971), which made him a superstar, remains one of his most popular films. Ironically, he was not the first choice: Frank Sinatra and Paul Newman, bigger names at the box office, were preferred. Though there were many who found the violence horrific and gratuitous, the violence was an integral part, making a serious comment on law and order. Harry stood for vigilante justice. His actions were condoned by his audience, who identified with him, rather than his critics, who accused Harry of being vicious, sexist, racist, fascist and the film of being an attack on liberal values and propaganda for para-legal police powers. The police liked what they saw and invited Clint Eastwood to speak at one of their gatherings.

Clint Eastwood in
The Outlaw Josey Wales

11

John Sturges (who had directed *Bad Day at Black Rock* and *The Magnificent Seven* so successfully) failed to make *Joe Kidd* (1972) work and it remained a dull, rambling Western. Vastly superior was *High Plains Drifter* (1972), a ghostly Western, which he directed himself, after he had sacked the original director, Philip Kaufman, who had written the screenplay. He was excellent as an archangel of death and retribution. *High Plains Drifter*, stylish and stylized, was one of the best Westerns of the 1970s, though few would have been able to guess this from reading the reviews at the time. Eastwood then went on to direct William Holden in *Breezy* (1973), a love story, in which he did not appear.

The critics were not so wild about Harry and *Magnum Force* (1973), many of them feeling that it didn't have either the style or the narrative energy of the original. On the other hand, *Thunderbolt and Lightfoot* (1974), a modern-day crime story, written and directed by Michael Cimino making his directorial debut at 31, was a perceptive comedy. Cimino had sent the script to Eastwood saying he could have it, but only if he were allowed to direct it.

The Eiger Sanction (1975), a badly scripted mountain spy thriller, variously described as 'time-passing rubbish', 'appalling tripe' and 'a good film to sleep to', was also (to quote one of the script's many mechanical lines) 'too shabby to be called cheap'. The actors played a secondary role to the Alps. However, with the release of *The Outlaw Josey Wales* (1976), it was obvious, even to his detractors, that Eastwood was a major talent both as a director and as an actor. This sombre story of vengeance and reconciliation, a personal favourite of his, was one of the best films of the 1970s.

The Enforcer (1976, not to be confused with the 1951 Humphrey Bogart movie of the same name) was advertised as the dirtiest Harry of them all. It was, in fact, the poorest of the three, routine stuff, a pale carbon copy of the original. In *The Gauntlet* (1977) he played a disillusioned, disreputable cop, well past his sell-by date. The only thing wrong with the casting was that he never actually looked like the loser he was meant to be playing; he still looked like Dirty Harry.

Every Which Way But Loose (1978) was mindless violence masquerading as macho fun and a big disappointment to everybody, except the general public, who turned up in large numbers to see it. Such was its success that two years later there was a revamp, *Any Which Way You Can* (1980), even more juvenile, and it, too, proved hugely popular.

Clint Eastwood in
The Enforcer

Don Siegel had a simple and gripping story to tell in *Escape from Alcatraz* (1979) and he told it in a straightforward, methodical, low-key manner, midway between the Warner Brothers prison dramas of the 1930s and Robert Bresson's *Un Condamné à mort s'est échappé* of the 1950s. Eastwood, understated yet eloquent, gave one of his most powerful performances.

Bronco Billy (1980), a modest, nostalgic movie with a light and engaging touch, felt like a wacky 1930s screwball comedy. Eastwood played a kiddywink cowboy, living in a dream world. The critics were disarmed; the film was a commercial failure. *Honkytonk Man* (1982), gentle, likeable and bittersweet, also received high praise, but it didn't do well at the box office, either. Eastwood may have liked playing losers, but his fans didn't like seeing him playing losers and they certainly didn't want to witness him having a death scene second only to Marguerite Gautier. Eastwood would say later that it was films like *Bronco Billy* and *Honkytonk Man* that gave him the confidence to make *Unforgiven*.

Firefox (1982), a lethargic, tacky, Cold War spy thriller, was so bad that it produced loud laughter at the press show and all the way to the bank. *Sudden Impact* (1983), the fourth Dirty Harry film, was excellently scripted and tightly directed; though, once again, the brutality, the right-wing moralizing and the vigilante justice were not to everybody's liking.

He played a cop with a taste for rough sex, morally corrupted by his job, in *Tightrope* (1984), another first-class adult thriller, one of his best films, popular with fans and critics alike, admired for its candour and bravery, even if there were objections to what were perceived to be its voyeurism and misogyny.

City Heat (1984), a pastiche 1930s gumshoe movie, in which he joined forces with Burt Reynolds, got a luke-warm response, the critics generally finding it a tedious romp and rejecting it as 'botched, superannuated Butch Cassidy and Sundance Kid'.

Eastwood, reared on Westerns and having a particular liking for William Wellman's *The Ox-Bow Incident*, Howard Hawks's *Red River* and the films of Anthony Mann, has always thought the genre not only good entertainment but a good way to put over a message. In 1985, with *Pale Rider*, he made a conscious effort to revive the Western (which had fallen out of favour), feeling it was the right moment to explore its classic mythology and spirit.

Clint Eastwood in
Unforgiven

14

There were those who thought *Heartbreak Ridge* (1986) the most gung-ho movie since John Wayne's *Sands of Iwo Jima*. 'Welcome to Camp Cliché!' said the wits; but Eastwood's performance as a truculent, disillusioned, old combat veteran, at odds in the modern world, was one of his most impressive characterizations.

Eastwood had been a jazz aficionado from an early age. *Bird* (1988), an unsentimental yet humane account of saxophonist Charlie Parker's harrowing life, was a labour of love, making no concessions whatsoever to the box office. Despite having a superb soundtrack and being one of the best films ever made about jazz, *Bird* did not prove popular with either black or white audiences. Black cinemagoers, in particular, criticized it for not addressing itself to racism and the pressure of being black in a white world.

In 1987, he slipped out of the polls for the first time (having been ranked among the top 10 box-office stars for 17 years, an amazing record) and he stayed out with the release of two mediocre thrillers, *The Dead Pool* (1988) and *Pink Cadillac* (1989). Much more worth while, yet no more successful at the box office, was the ecologically timely *White Hunter, Black Heart* (1990), though it was never meant to be an anti-hunting statement. Peter Viertel's screenplay (based on director John Huston's fixation to shoot an elephant) was highly literate; rarely has Eastwood had to speak so many lines. Both the film and his performance were underrated.

In the hope of reaching a younger market, he teamed up with Charlie Sheen (who had just had a big hit with *Young Guns*) to make *The Rookie* (1990), which was no more successful than *The Dead Pool* and *Pink Cadillac* had been. 'Back on the trash track,' said the *Mail on Sunday*. 'Astonishingly inadequate piece of piffle,' said *Time Out*. 'Pretty dire slice of video fodder,' said the *Daily Telegraph*.

He made a stunning comeback in 1992. *Unforgiven* (not to be confused with the 1960 John Huston film of the same name) shattered box-office records and went on to win four Academy awards, including best picture, best director, best supporting actor (Gene Hackman) and best editing (Joel Cox). All that was missing was the award for best actor; Eastwood lost out to Al Pacino in *Scent of a Woman*. The movie made a strong statement condemning violence by describing it in graphic and brutal detail. Some saw the film as an apologia (strongly denied) for the violence in the earlier movies. Eastwood has said that if *Unforgiven* were to prove to be his final Western, then it would be the perfect Western for him.

In the Line of Fire (1993), directed by Wolfgang Petersen (whose submarine saga, *Das Boot*, Eastwood had much admired) was an exciting and well-written political thriller and a first-rate vehicle for him and John Malkovich. He then, generously, played a supporting role to Kevin Costner in *A Perfect World*. His latest film is *The Bridges of Madison County*, opposite Meryl Streep.

Few people in the film business have made so great an impact and for so long as Clint Eastwood. The pages which follow are a record of and a tribute to his magnetism as an actor, his professionalism as a director and his business acumen as a producer. He works with the same repertory of people again and again. His movies are famous for coming in on time and under budget. Now in his mid-sixties, he continues to maintain a shrewd balancing act between the movies he makes for commercial reasons and the movies he makes for himself. It is not always as easy to separate the two as might be thought.

The 1950s

FRANCIS IN THE NAVY

Directed by Arthur Lubin   1955

Francis was a talking mule and *Francis in the Navy* was the sixth in the series of his adventures. Donald O'Connor played two roles – bumbling idiot and war hero – and didn't get to sing or dance in either. Clint Eastwood played one of the sailors.

The jawing of a jackass is one of nature's most unlovely sounds and *Francis in the Navy* proves it.

Oscar Godbout, *New York Times*

Donald O'Connor,
Clint Eastwood and
Francis Genks in
Francis in the Navy

THE FIRST TRAVELING SALESLADY

Directed by Arthur Lubin   1956

An emancipated saleslady (Ginger Rogers), who had gone bankrupt selling corsets, decided to head west in 1897 and sell barbed wire to the Texans instead. She was accompanied by her partner, an ex-chorus girl (stage comedienne Carol Channing), who got to growl an indifferent song, 'A corset can do a lot for a lady because it helps to show what a lady's got'.

Clint Eastwood headed the featured players, cast as a very shy and very handsome rough rider, a US cavalry of one, who met the ex-chorus girl while he was manning a recruiting desk in a hotel foyer. 'Do you like girls?' she asked. 'Yes, mam, I do.' A handful of scenes followed. Eastwood, who was a bit young to be playing her suitor, proposed off-screen. *The First Traveling Saleslady* should have been a full-scale musical.

Clint Eastwood is very attractive as Carol Channing's beau.

Hollywood Reporter

Clint Eastwood and Carol Channing in *The First Traveling Saleslady*

AMBUSH AT CIMARRON PASS

Directed by Jodie Copelan   1957

Clint Eastwood has been quoted as describing this low-budget Western as 'the lousiest Western ever made'. He was cast as a member of a gang who ambushed a group of ex-Confederate soldiers. Unwilling to accept the South's defeat in the American Civil War, he was all in favour of killing them. In between fighting the Apaches, he found time to have a fight with the sergeant (Scott Brady) over the heroine (Margia Dean).

Fine portrayals also come from Margia Dean, Frank Gestle, Clint Eastwood and Dirk London.

Variety

Scott Brady and Clint Eastwood in *Ambush at Cimarron Pass*

RAWHIDE

1959-1966

Clint Eastwood in
Rawhide

Margaret O'Brien, Mercedes McCambridge, Victor McLaglen, Cesar Romero, Neville Brand, Peter Lorre, Agnes Moorehead, Woody Strode, E.G. Marshall, Mary Astor, John Cassevetes, Zachary Scott, Brian Aherne, Barbara Stanwyck, James Coburn, Walter Pidgeon, John Ireland, Claude Rains, Walter Slezak, Frankie Avalon, Mickey Rooney, Warren Oates, Lee Van Cleef, Dean Martin, Rip Torn and Charles Bronson. Frankie Laine, who sang the theme song, also made a guest appearance.

Eastwood would later invite one of the directors, Ted Post, to direct him in *Hang 'Em High* and *Magnum Force*.

I would rate veteran actor Eric Fleming and ex-lumberjack Clint Eastwood, the men in charge of driving the herds, the only two Western stars outside of *Wagon Train* apparently able to act and move the muscles of their faces at the same time.

James Thomas, *Daily Express*

They were fun years and they were frustrating, too . . . I was pigeon-holed as an actor. It was pretty restrictive, but I sure learned a lot.

Clint Eastwood

Move 'em on, head 'em up, head 'em up, move 'em on. *Rawhide*, the whip-cracking story of a long (very long) cattledrive from San Antonio, Texas, to Sedalia, Kansas, kept rollin', rollin', rollin' for 217 episodes to become one of the most popular television Western series ever. The scripts, praised for their authenticity, were loosely based on the diary of a real-life cattle drover who lived in the 1860s.

Clint Eastwood, one of the few regulars to remain with the show for its entire run, played the young and impetuous second-in-command, ramrod Rowdy Yates, until 1965 when Rowdy became the trail boss and he took over the leading role from Eric Fleming.

The series employed any number of guest stars, including Dan Duryea, Brian Donlevy,

Clint Eastwood in
Rawhide

The 1960s

PER UN PUGNO DI DOLLARI

Directed by Sergio Leone   1964
English title: *A Fistful of Dollars*

You ask most people what they were about and they can't tell you, but they can tell you the look.

Clint Eastwood

The story of *A Fistful of Dollars*, a low-budget spaghetti Western, was borrowed from one of Clint Eastwood's favourite movies, Akira Kurosawa's *Yojimbo*, the Samurai classic, starring the great Japanese actor Toshiro Mifune. The result was that the film was not released in the US for three years due to copyright problems.

An anonymous Stranger arrived in a small Mexican town. It was the sort of place where you only got respect by killing other men. The body count was high and the coffin-maker was kept busy. The Stranger was tall (6′ 4″), lean, good-looking, enigmatic and he wore a poncho. (The poncho immediately became all the rage with Italian young men.) His hat was pulled down over his eyes. He smoked thin black cigars; the half-smoked cheroot in the corner of his mouth was his trademark. Cool, intelligent, soft-spoken, polite, steely, he stared hard and kept his eyes skint. He was quick on the draw and he had a laconic sense of humour. He would open a door. 'Hello!' he would say and shoot five men dead.

The Man With No Name (actually his name was Joe) was a new type of hero, cold-blooded and unscrupulous, a symbolic figure, who displayed no emotion and was immune to the cries of children and women. Honour and morality were not part of his baggage. He looked mean. He was mean. He had barely arrived in the town before he was ordering three coffins.

The story was banal melodrama. Two rival families were locked in a bitter feud. Joe hired himself out to both, playing them off against each other. He was so badly beaten up at one point that it became absurd he could carry on. The violence was graphic, the dialogue stilted and the dubbing atrocious. The production was shot in Spain. ('Pity it wasn't buried there,' said *Time* magazine.)

The cowboys were laughing sadists, much given to torture, vicious beatings, whippings, kickings, stringing up old men and hammy acting. There were so many close-ups of their faces, it was like flicking through an actors' directory. Eastwood got his effects by remaining impassive. Some people, including the Italian producers, thought he wasn't acting.

The final showdown in the empty square was classic Hollywood Western, with the hero taking on all the bad guys single-handed. Eastwood was given a dramatic entrance, silhouetted against a smoking building which had just been dynamited, his entrance directly lifted from *Yojimbo*. As he advanced, the leading villain (Gian Maria Volonté) shot him down not once, not twice, not thrice, not four but five times and each time Joe got up and kept advancing. The man was indestructible. (Well, actually, he was wearing armour plating.)

Sergio Leone's approach to the Western may have been tongue-in-cheek, but his use of the wide screen, with its unusual camera angles, and the enormous close-ups of faces, eyes, guns, boots and spurs, had tremendous visual flair. Ennio Morricone's distinctive, twanging score was very much part of the film's success.

José Calvo and
Clint Eastwood in
A Fistful of Dollars

The calculated sadism of the film would be offensive were it not for the neutralizing laughter aroused by the ludicrousness of the whole exercise.

Philip French, *Observer*

The most unnecessarily violent film I can remember. If this is parody, it needs to be a good deal lighter on the trigger.

Felix Barker, *Evening News*

The only thing that could possibly explain why such a film made a killing at the Italian and UK box offices is the amount of killing that goes on in it.

Alexander Walker, *Evening Standard*

Eastwood as the stranger makes full use of his one expression.

Hollis Alpert, *Saturday Review*

Sergio Leone has a certain gift for striking compositions. But the overall effect is hardly such as to set the Thames on fire, whatever it did to the Tiber.

John Russell Taylor, *The Times*

He is a morbid, amusing, campy fraud.

Bosley Crowther, *New York Times*

Has all the psychological depth of Bugs Bunny.

Ian Christie, *Daily Express*

José Calvo and
Clint Eastwood in
A Fistful of Dollars

PER QUALCHE DOLLARI IN PIÙ

Directed by Sergio Leone   1965
English title: *For a Few Dollars More*

Where life had no value, death, sometimes, had its price. That is why bounty killers appeared.

Legend

A horseman advanced. Off-screen a man hummed and loaded his rifle. The advancing horseman was shot dead. The horse bolted. The credit titles began, accompanied by the whistling, jolly gunfire and male choir first heard during the credits for *A Fistful of Dollars*.

There were two bounty hunters. The first was Colonel Douglas Mortimer (Lee Van Cleef), a former Confederate officer, who looked evil but wasn't. He was out only to avenge the rape and suicide of his sister and the murder of her young husband. The second hunter was a cold, amoral gangster (Clint Eastwood), a sharp-eyed opportunist, solely in it for the money. Mortimer, more mature, classier, recognized in the younger man his younger, reckless self. There was a jokey encounter early on when the two men, showing off, gave a display of their shooting skills, shooting each other's hats.

Eastwood had a good first entrance in the pouring rain. First the poncho, then the cigar, then the hat and only finally the bearded face. The Man With No Name (formerly Joe, now Manco) had youth and cheek, delivering dynamite to prison with a smile, his appearance at the barred window heralded by the smoke of his cigar. 'He's nothing but a wild, vicious animal,' said a nervous hotel manager. 'He's tall, isn't he?' gushed the bosomy receptionist, thrilled to hear he didn't wear long johns. (The film didn't confirm whether this was true or not.) Eastwood, once again, wisely, left 'the acting' to the Italians, who went in for big, operatic performances.

Clint Eastwood in *For a Few Dollars More*

Lee Van Cleef, Clint Eastwood and Gian Maria Volonté in *For a Few Dollars More*

The story concerned a robbery of a bank. The bounty hunters joined forces to kill the robbers and to take the loot for themselves. The villain was Indio, a deranged drug addict and murderer, who enjoyed torturing his victims and addressing his gang from the pulpit of a ruined church. Ennio Morricone's music scored his hysteria and gave him a haunting tune to soothe his jangled nerves, which was played every time he opened a locket watch he had stolen from Mortimer's sister. Indio was played by Gian Maria Volonté, perfect casting for a villain in a Jacobean melodrama. Klaus Kinski appeared as one of his twitching henchmen, a hunchback on whose hunch Van Cleef, so memorably, struck a match.

Sergio Leone, never subtle, plunged cinemagoers into a raucous bloodbath. The

Clint Eastwood and Gian Maria Volonté in *For a Few Dollars More*

screen was littered with corpses, the massacre of the prison guards complementing the massacre of the ambushed soldiers in *A Fistful of Dollars*. In a world where life depended on the gun, The Man With No Name could outdraw anybody and, in the final sequence, he counted the dead bodies, piled high in his wagon, in terms of hundreds of dollars.

The film veers to what you would call the pornography of violence.

Alexander Walker, *Evening Standard*

It is the meat of sadistic morons.

Felix Barker, *Evening News*

Enough gratuitous violence to satisfy a concentration commandant.

Ian Christie, *Daily Express*

Sergio Leone keeps the style somewhere just short of burlesque.

Patrick Gibbs, *Daily Telegraph*

For those who like an elemental Western with galvanic gestures, a twanging score full of Jew's harps and choral chanting, and a lofty disdain for sense and authenticity, the film will be ideal.

Time

The two American stars (Clint Eastwood and Lee Van Cleef) are used more for their looks than as actors.

David Robinson, *Financial Times*

IL BUONO, IL BRUTTO, IL CATTIVO

Directed by Sergio Leone   1966
English title: *The Good, the Bad and the Ugly*

I don't want to be remembered as a philosopher, unlike so many of my celluloid brothers. I want to be remembered as an entertainer – or forget me.

Sergio Leone

The Good was Blondy, played by Clint Eastwood, the Bad was Angel Eyes, played by Lee Van Cleef, and the Ugly was Tuco, played by Eli Wallach. The wags said the title referred to the camerawork, the acting and the violence. The title, admittedly, was ironic. All three men were bad, keen to lay their hands on a Confederate cashbox hidden in a cemetery. It was ages before anybody spoke and when they did, it was the usual awful dubbing.

Eastwood had a long-delayed first entrance. He was his familiar, anonymous, casually assured self, bemused by what was going on around him. He smiled. He squinted. (Eastwood would say later that if he ever lost his squint, 'his career would go down the tubes'.) He never raised his voice. He could recognize a man by his gunfire: 'Every gun makes its own tune.' If anybody wanted to find him, they just followed a trail of cigar butts.

Blondy had formed a partnership with Tuco, a Mexican bandit. The idea was that he would capture Tuco, hand him over to the law, collect the bounty, wait until the noose was round Tuco's neck and then, just as he was about to be hung, he would shoot the rope and they would make their escape on Blondy's horse. They would then go on to the next town and repeat the process, splitting the reward. One day Blondy thought it was no longer worth his while and he left Tuco to die in the desert. Tuco was not amused.

Tuco was a greasy, cunning, greedy, treacherous, lying rat who had committed such a catalogue of crimes that it was funny just to listen to the sheriff reading them out: murder, robbery, extortion, rape, arson, perjury, pimping, kidnapping . . . You name it, he'd done it. Wallach, a wonderfully comic villain, had all the best scenes: robbing a gunsmith; pleading with Blondy not to die ('Please don't die, I'm your friend'); pleading with a dying Confederate soldier to reveal the location of the grave; and sitting in his bath, calmly killing his would-be assassin with a gun hidden under the soap suds and offering some good, if belated, advice: 'When you have to shoot, shoot, don't talk.'

Tuco had one serious scene with his brother, whom he accused of cowardice and deserting their parents. For a man who didn't want to die of poverty in Mexico, there were, evidently, only two options. He could become either a bandit or a priest. His brother had chosen to become a priest.

There was a good old-fashioned scene, well edited, when Blondy was in his hotel bedroom and the noise of the soldiers marching by in the street drowned the sound of three assassins climbing the staircase. There was an electrifying moment when the soldiers came to a halt and Blondy was suddenly aware of the men on the landing outside his door.

The story was set during the American Civil War and the screenplay had as many climaxes as a Victorian novel awaiting serialization. Just as Tuco was about to kill Blondy, a bomb destroyed the hotel. Just as Tuco was about to kill Blondy for the second time, a driverless coach, full of dead and dying Confederate

Eli Wallach and Clint
Eastwood in *The Good,
the Bad and the Ugly*

soldiers, arrived (an extraordinarily eerie
moment, this). Just as they were making their
getaway, they mistook Confederate soldiers for
Yankees and were arrested; the mistake was
understandable, as the dust of the desert had
turned the soldiers' dark blue tunics light blue.

The Civil War gave the story its bitterness
and cynicism; it also gave it its dignity and
tragedy. The battlefield had an epic sweep, the
trenches recalling the trenches of World War I.
Though there were some schoolboy heroics,
with Blondy and Tuco blowing up a bridge, the
war was there essentially to register the
appalling waste of life.

The scenes in the POW camp were a grim
replay of the war crimes at the notorious camp
at Andersonville. Angel Eyes was cast as a
sadistic torturer and murderer, the agony of the
soldiers underlined by Ennio Morricone's
shrieking score. The prison band was forced to
play to drown the screams, and the tune they
played was especially haunting. It was a
sequence to recall the band that had been
forced to play during World War II in the Nazi
concentration camp as the Jews were marched
off to the gas chambers.

The Good, the Bad and the Ugly was filmed
in a variety of magnificent outdoor settings. A
familiar Western scene – a shoot-out in a
deserted town – was given a new lease of death
by taking place while the town was being
bombed and its streets and alleys were filled
with smoke. The sequence was wittily acted
and wittily scored.

Towards the end of the film Blondy gave his
coat to a dying soldier, a good action totally out
of character and there only, so it seemed, in
order for Eastwood to put on his poncho and

Lee Van Cleef, Eli Wallach
and Clint Eastwood
in *The Good, the Bad and
the Ugly*

become The Man With No Name for a memorable and breathtaking climax, a three-cornered
shoot-out in a ring at the very centre of a
massive cemetery for the war dead. The
measure of a man in a Western has always been
his ability to shoot faster than the other fellow,
but the question here was who did you shoot
first? Leone built up the pressure in his
characteristic manner by endless delays with
bold close-ups of faces, eyes and hands moving
to triggers. Morricone quoted the locket-watch
tune he had used in *For a Few Dollars More*.

There were those who thought Blondy a
cardboard comic-strip hero, but there was
nothing either cardboard or comic strip about
Eastwood's cool and understated performance.

**A curious amalgam of the visually striking, the
dramatically feeble and the offensively sadistic.**

Variety

**Presumably the savagery is another sign of the
times.**

Dilys Powell, *Sunday Times*

**Deaths are numerous, violent and lingered on – and
the Western itself is one of the victims.**

David Wilson, *Guardian*

**Those Italian Westerns with Clint Eastwood
chewing his cheroot and acting with as much
expression as a man with neuralgia are really the
bitter end.**

Dick Richards, *Daily Mirror*

**Must be the most expensive, pious and repellent
movie in the history of its peculiar genre.**

Renata Adler, *New York Times*

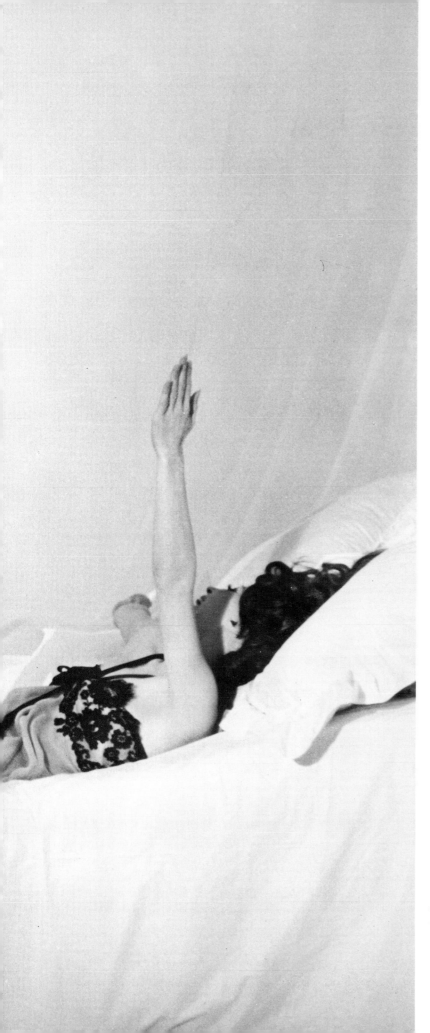

LE STREGHE

Directed by Vittorio de Sica   1966
English title: *The Witches*

Le Streghe was divided into five episodes.
Eastwood appeared in the last, *Una sera come
le altre* (*A Night Like Any Other*), which
described the fantasies of a housewife (Silvana
Mangano), who was bored with her husband
(Clint Eastwood), who was too tired to do
anything but sleep when he came home from
work.

**The piece gives Mr Eastwood nothing much to do
but look patient.**

Vincent Canby, *New York Times*

Clint Eastwood and
Silvana Mangano in
The Witches

HANG 'EM HIGH

Directed by Ted Post   1968

Jed Cooper, an ex-lawman, was driving a herd of cattle. The next minute he was being lassoed, dragged through a river, strung up and the credit titles hadn't even begun. He was accused of being a rustler and a murderer. Despite pleading his innocence he was lynched and left for dead. A passing marshal saved his life. *Hang 'Em High* was never as good again.

The hanging left a nasty scar and not just on Jed's neck. Invited by Judge Fenton to become his deputy, he accepted the badge, but only so that he could exact his revenge. He spent the rest of the movie tracking down his lynchers.

The central event was a public hanging, turned into a holiday by the town and given the full carnival atmosphere, with families coming from miles around, bringing the children. A young preacher led the assembled crowd in community hymn singing, while the camera lingered over the black hoods, the adjusted nooses, the sandbags, the trapdoors and the hands ready to trigger the final drop. The gallows were an exact replica of the original gallows built to hang 12 men simultaneously, scaled down to six-men size. Dominic Frontière's score, heavy and melodramatic, provided a brass percussion chime replica of the sound of a scaffold being tripped. Some critics found the detail too morbid. 'Strictly for ghouls!' was the *Daily Mirror* headline.

Jed (a far more heroic character than The Man With No Name, even if he was liable to stub out his cigar in a cowboy's beer) disapproved of the mass hangings, arguing that the men might just as well have been lynched. The judge contended that there was a difference between being lynched and being judged and if he didn't know the difference he had better hand in his badge. It was interesting that Jed should argue for mercy while he was vigorously pursuing his personal vendetta. Clint Eastwood, acting with flinty certitude, dealt with the ambiguity by simply ignoring it.

Judge Fenton was based on the real-life hanging Judge Parker, the only representative of US law in the Oklahoma Territory in 1873. 'I'm the law,' he said. 'All the law.' Fenton, who had to cover 70,000 miles with nine marshals and only one courthouse, wanted the territory to become a state and he knew that so long as the lawlessness continued, it wouldn't. His jails overflowed.

Fenton had a genuine affection for his protégé and, after one successful sortie, had rewarded him with a freebie in the local brothel. His behaviour in his own courtroom, however, made many people feel it was he who should be locked up. Pat Hingle found it difficult to reconcile the two sides of the judge's character: the folksiness on the one hand and the mercilessness on the other.

A romantic interest was dragged in. There was a widow (Inger Stevens) who was looking for the men who had killed her husband and raped her. It was she who nursed Jed back to health after he had been shot. They shared a sentimental picnic during which she allowed him just two kisses. A storm came up. Jed collapsed and they took shelter in a log-cabin conveniently nearby, where she gave him a good rub before lying next to him to keep him warm. The camera, tactfully, stayed outside the cabin all night.

There was also a second woman, a jolly prostitute (Arlene Golonka). Rather than watch

Clint Eastwood in
Hang 'Em High

Arlene Golonka and
Clint Eastwood in
Hang 'Em High

Eastwood on the Rawhide series. *Hang 'Em High* was his feature debut and it felt like an efficient television movie without the commercial breaks.

Eastwood has made his first talking picture.

Ian Christie, *Daily Express*

Hang 'Em High **comes across as a poor American-made imitation of a poor Italian-made imitation of an American Western . . . Eastwood projects a likable image, but the part is only a shade more developed over his Sergio Leone Italoators. Some change of pace is sorely needed, lest he become typed.**

Variety

It must be said that, as an actor, Clint Eastwood has perfected the sound of silence, which is quite impressive at times.

Margaret Hinxman, *Sunday Telegraph*

Films grow steadily more violent, and will continue to do so unless we apply the obvious remedy. Stay away.

Felix Barker, *Evening News*

Most unfortunate of all, Mr Eastwood, with his glum sincerity, isn't much of an actor.

Howard Thompson, *New York Times*

the hangings, Jed got drunk and dragged her off for a quickie, during the singing of 'Rock of Ages', which was so quick, it was all over before the crowd had finished singing the last verse.

Ed Begley was cast as the wealthy ranch owner who had headed the unauthorized posse. Essentially a decent fellow, he realized too late that, if you hanged an innocent man by mistake, you should make certain that you finished off the job. Begley had a good scene right at the end when he was all alone in his house, a frightened old man, his two henchmen having just been killed. Running out of ammunition, he shut the door. By the time Jed had climbed the stairs, walked down the landing, tried a few doors and found the right room, he had had time to hang himself.

The director, Ted Post, had worked with

COOGAN'S BLUFF

Directed by Don Siegel   1968

He insists on being an anti-hero. I've never worked with an actor who was less conscious of his good image.

Don Siegel

Coogan's Bluff, well-made, fast-moving, was that rare thing, an urban Western, probably the first Western to be set in modern New York. An Arizonian deputy sheriff was put among the metropolitan policemen. The contrast between their more sophisticated approach and his frontier-style policing offered opportunities for dry humour at his expense and also at the expense of the big city and its liberal attitudes.

Deputy Sheriff Coogan (Clint Eastwood), a loner, tough and stubborn, was an instinctive hunter and his character was established in the opening sequence in the Arizona desert when he arrested a renegade Indian (Rudy Diaz) he had been tracking for three days and tied him up on the porch of the house of a local whore, while he had a bath and sex. The Indian was treated as if he were an animal, no different from any other blood sport. Compassion and humanity were low on Coogan's list of priorities; the last time he had shown pity for a criminal he had ended up with a six-inch blade in his gut.

He was sent to New York to extradite a prisoner, a murderer. Outside his territory, the sheriff cut a comic figure in his brown suit, stetson, bootlace tie and boots with the pointed toes. Tall, tanned and incredibly good-looking, he was so like everybody's idea of a cowboy that everybody instantly presumed he was from Texas and fair game. Cab drivers, hotel clerks and prostitutes tried to take him for a ride. One whore, whose advances he turned down,

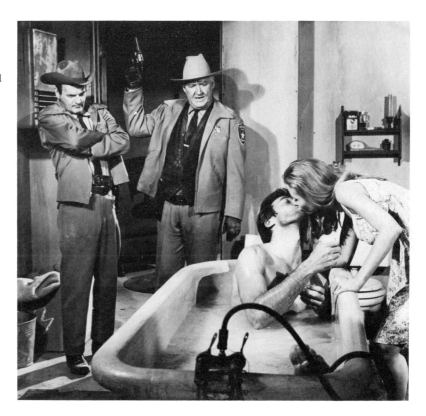

Tom Tully, Clint Eastwood and Melodie Johnson in *Coogan's Bluff*

thought she could steal his wallet and when she found she couldn't, she was so mad, all she could do was scream, 'Texas faggot!'

The murderer, James Ringerman (Don Stroud), was in a prison hospital, recovering from an LSD trip. Coogan, accustomed to direct action, took matters into his own hands, cutting through the red tape, ignoring District Office. Having bluffed a doctor into handing Ringerman over, he was then zapped into unconsciousness at the airport. The prisoner escaped and he was taken off the case. Feeling that his reputation was on the line, he simply disregarded the order. (A man's gotta do what he's gotta do.)

47

Clint Eastwood in
Coogan's Bluff

Lee J. Cobb, wearing a hat to hide his baldness, was cast as a tired, cynical, disenchanted detective who, hamstrung by his bosses, had to do everything by the book. 'This isn't the OK Corral,' he reminded Coogan in one of their many confrontations, exasperated by his arrogance.

Don Siegel captured the underworld in action in a poolroom when Coogan, taking on nine men wielding cues, suffered a terrible beating, the sort of martyrdom cinemagoers had come to expect from Marlon Brando in his films. A psychedelic experience which followed in an overcrowded discotheque (125 extras plus 400 genuine hippies) was overlong, but it allowed Coogan to get involved with a minder and have a characteristic, laconic exchange: 'I don't like violence,' he admitted, parodying the traditional, American tough guy. 'You drop that blade or you won't believe what happens next, even when it's happened.' The man, naturally, dropped his knife.

The climax took place in the cloisters and grounds of Fort Tryon Park, an urban parkland, with Coogan chasing after Ringerman. The sequence complemented the opening, the camera looking down on the action, through the trees, almost as if the sheriff were hunting prey back in Arizona. The chase, on motorcycles, along paths and up and down steps, ended with Coogan forcing Ringerman to collide with him. 'I'm making a citizen's arrest!' he yelled, hurling the thug at the detective's feet, the detective having arrived, as regular filmgoers would expect, only when it was all over.

Eastwood managed to remain likeable even when the sheriff's behaviour to prisoners and

Clint Eastwood in
Coogan's Bluff

women was despicable. However, what gave
the role an extra significance was his regret for
the passing of rural America. There was a key
scene when he was looking at a panoramic
view of New York, trying to picture the way it
had been before people had come along and
fouled it up.

Susan Clark was cast as a softly spoken
probation officer who humanized him. The
foreplay was nicely judged by Eastwood, who
acted with gentle, sexy humour. Don Stroud
and Rudy Diaz had obviously been cast as the
fugitives because they had the same sort of
features. Ringerman's hippie girlfriend (Tisha
Sterling) was a ding-dong bore. A much more
interesting character was Ringerman's nutty
mother. Betty Field had only one scene and she
made the most of it.

**And suddenly Mr Eastwood, released from the
crudity of the Italian imitations, moves with the
cool, deliberate elegance of the real thing. At last he
looks like the true Western hero.**

Dick Richards, *Daily Mirror*

**Eastwood, who hitherto displayed nothing more
than a capacity for iron-jawed belligerency in a
series of Italian-made Westerns, performs with a
measure of real feeling in the role that fits him as
comfortably as his tooled leather boots.**

Time

**Some may find the Eastwood character Fascist
beyond redemption, or at least beyond
identification, but in an American context, he is all
too believable, the cool, emotionless, slightly
sadistic man of the sixties.**

Richard Roud, *Guardian*

WHERE EAGLES DARE

Directed by Brian G. Hutton   1968

Richard Burton and I killed so many Nazis in two hours, it made me wonder why the war took so long.

Clint Eastwood, quoted by Maureen Dowd,
New York Times

Alistair MacLean's *Where Eagles Dare*, built on the same lines as his *The Guns of Navarone*, was an action-packed espionage thriller, a ripping yarn, full of death-defying feats and no characterization whatsoever.

Major John Smith (Richard Burton) was given the mission of rescuing an imprisoned American general from the impregnable and inaccessible Schloss Adler – the Castle of the Eagle – mountain headquarters of the German Secret Service and Gestapo in south Germany during World War II. His team included an American, Lieutenant Morris Schaffer (Clint Eastwood), a woman (Mary Ure) and four others. It wasn't exactly a perfect team. Three out of the seven turned out to be traitors. 'The whole operation looks impossible,' moaned Michael Hordern, back in London, in his role of Naval Intelligence officer. 'The Germans have totally penetrated MI6.' (The dialogue was not the film's strong point.) A game of double bluff was played by double agents doubling all over the place; even the American general they were meant to be rescuing turned out to be an ex-actor (Robert Beatty) impersonating the general.

'You shouldn't go on these insane missions; you're getting too old,' observed the woman team member to Smith. 'See you in the woodshed,' he replied. Evidently, they'd been on missions together before. Much publicity was made of Burton letting down his hair and

Ingrid Pitt, Clint Eastwood, Mary Ure and Richard Burton in *Where Eagles Dare*

taking a holiday from his more serious work. It was reported that he had made the film to please his children. 'Why do you always get killed?' they had asked. 'Why don't you do a picture in which you do the killing?'

There was certainly a lot of cold-blooded shooting and the production went with a bang. Castle, buildings, bridges, trees, trucks, cars, motorbikes, airports were all blown up. It was a big-budget movie and no expense was spared. By the end of the picture there wasn't a German left alive. In fact, the Germans were there just so Smith and Schaffer could mow them down.

The storyline was so wildly improbable and so ridiculously complicated that even those participating didn't know what was going on.

Richard Burton and
Clint Eastwood in
Where Eagles Dare

A bit of old-fashioned, schoolboy excitement
was provided by a desperate fight in, round
and on top of a moving cable car, but for the
most part the action was devoid of drama, wit
and tension. The legendary stuntman Yakima
Canutt (who had organized the chariot race in
Ben Hur) was responsible for the technically
impressive final sequence, which had plenty of
pace, but the feats and odds were so
preposterous, they ceased to be hair-raising.

Lieutenant Schaffer of the American Rangers
was a professional killer. Like everybody else
in the cast, he played a supporting role to the
bullets and dynamite explosions. Eastwood
trudged through snow, scaled castle walls and
blasted anything and everything with his
machine-gun. 'Hello!' he would say before he
shot or knifed somebody. 'Hello!' was a

Clint Eastwood in
Where Eagles Dare

running gag. (He had said 'Hello!' in *A Fistful
of Dollars*, too.) There wasn't much acting to be
done. Eastwood took second billing and let
Burton do all the talking.

The German officers were played by Anton
Diffring, Ferdy Mayne and Derren Nesbitt.
Diffring rarely played anything else but German
officers. Mayne sported a monocle and Nesbitt
played a nasty ginger-haired Gestapo. Patrick
Wymark was a campy, treacherous Brit. He
made his exit from a plane while it was flying
over the Alps. As he stood in the open
doorway, it looked for a moment as if he was
about to say, 'I'm going outside and may be
gone for some time.'

**Eagle was a sophisticated, illogical film, a very
complicated story. I'm still not sure we quite figured
out the plot.**

Brian G. Hutton

**But it's the action that counts – and on this level
Where Eagles Dare is an undeniable success.**

Clive Hirshhorn, *Sunday Express*

No end of fun for stony-hearted boys.

Dilys Powell, *Sunday Times*

**It reaches such heights of absurdity, it is hootingly
funny. Do not resist it. Yield, uncritically, and it is
really quite enjoyable!**

Madeleine Harmsworth, *Daily Mirror*

**Clint is in the great line of Spencer Tracy and James
Stewart and Bob Mitchum. They have a kind of
dynamic lethargy. They appear to do nothing and
they do everything.**

Richard Burton, quoted by Jean Vallely, *Esquire*

PAINT YOUR WAGON

Directed by Joshua Logan   1969

Paramount had hoped to repeat the success of *The Sound of Music* and *My Fair Lady*; instead *Paint Your Wagon*, overblown, interminable and uncinematic, proved a costly failure, going way over budget.

Alan Jay Lerner and Frederick Loewe's musical Western had had a modest run on Broadway in 1951, but by the time it reached the screen in 1969 it was barely recognizable. It had a new book by Paddy Chayefsky and new music by André Previn, neither of which was distinguished.

The story was set during the Californian Gold Rush of the 1840s and traced the growth of a mining town, No Name City, from shanty town to boomtown. Its Sodom and Gomarrah-like destruction was the film's best and funniest sequence; its collapse caused, however, not by lust and corruption but by greedy prospectors tunnelling underneath it.

The highlight of the original Broadway show had been the choreography of Agnes de Mille. The movie had no choreography by either Agnes de Mille or anybody else for that matter. Joshua Logan left the chorus just standing and sitting around in a series of static tableaux during the songs, while the extras (behaving like a lot of extras) ran around, jumped about and waved their arms. What the movie desperately needed was the wit and energy Stanley Donen and Michael Kidd had brought to *Seven Brides for Seven Brothers*. Only the arrival of the whores ('There's a Coach Comin' in') gave the show a momentary lift. The best number remained the rousing opener, 'Paint Your Wagon', sung in a number of languages.

Lee Marvin and Clint Eastwood were chosen for their clout at the box office rather than their singing voices. Marvin, an untrained baritone, growled his way through 'Wand'rin' Star'. It was his most underplayed moment and the song, in Great Britain, went straight to the top of the charts. The only lead actor who was really able to sing was Harve Presnell (playing the gambler, Rotten Luck Willie) and he belted out 'They Call the Wind Maria' in the pouring rain.

The two leading characters were prospectors: the wild 49-year-old Ben Rumson and his young 'Pardner', who looked after him when he was drunk and melancholy. Marvin, always larger-than-life, worked hard for his laughs, recycling the Oscar-winning performance he had given in *Cat Ballou*. Top-hatted, white-haired, white-whiskered, sad-eyed, he looked comical in his red long johns and spent much of his time falling flat on his face.

The sentimental friendship was put to the test when Ben, in a drunken stupor, bought himself a wife off a Mormon (who had two wives), paying $800 for her in open auction. He invited 'Pardner' to share her with him. She, being a Mormon, had no difficulty in accepting a *ménage à trois*. 'I'm willing,' she said. 'I think it's a humane, practical, beautiful solution. I was married to a man who had two wives. Why can't I have two husbands?' They became a happily married triple. The producers, failing to get Julie Andrews after her enormous success in *The Sound of Music*, cast Jean Seberg, who had a Mormon-like steeliness, but she, too, was no singer.

Since Ben's wife was the only woman among 400 men in a 90-mile radius, the all-male community immediately voted in favour of prostitution and kidnapped six French whores.

Clint Eastwood, Jean
Seberg and Lee Marvin
in *Paint Your Wagon*

As Ben explained to a fresh-faced, churchgoing youth (Tom Ligon), if you didn't have a woman you could go blind. Fortunately, the youth had a natural talent for dissipation and was soon drinking, gambling, smoking and whoring with the best of them.

'Pardner', clean in mind and body, the decentest man Ben had ever known, neither drank nor gambled; he talked to the trees. He also sang 'I Still See Elisa', which was rather odd, since it had been Ben's song when *Paint Your Wagon* played in the theatre. An old man's remembrance about his wife was turned into a young man's fantasy about a girl he had never even seen. Eastwood's best number was 'Gold Fever' (one of the new songs), which at least made an effort to say something about what he and the town had become.

Eastwood, who built his reputation by speaking very little in a string of Italian-made Westerns, sings pleasantly enough but takes apart his reputation by speaking often and badly, as if the scriptgirl had neglected to give him each succeeding line.

Joseph Morgenstern, *Newsweek*

Compared with Marvin's agonized histrionics and the wild overplaying of most of the rest of the cast, Clint Eastwood preserves a certain uncomfortable dignity.

Penelope Mortimer, *Observer*

The stars have singing voices that would be assets to any bathroom.

Alexander Walker, *Evening Standard*

No music to my ears.

Arthur Knight, *Saturday Review* headline

TWO MULES FOR SISTER SARA

Directed by Don Siegel 1969

I won't reveal what Shirley MacLaine's real occupation is, but she's not the kind of girl you would be likely to take home to your mother's for tea.

Ian Christie, *Daily Express*

Two Mules for Sister Sara had a good story by Budd Boetticher, cult director of many classic B-movie Westerns in the late 1950s, and a witty, intelligent and funny screenplay by Albert Maltz. The action was set in French-occupied Mexico in 1865, during the Mexican revolution, at the time of Juárez and Maximilian. Clint Eastwood was cast as Hogan, a disillusioned veteran of the American Civil War, who earned his living as a mercenary, working for the Mexicans, hoping to make enough cash to open the best gambling saloon in San Francisco.

The action opened in long shot. Don Siegel explained later that the owl, big fish, jack rabbit, wild cat, rattlesnake and tarantula that Hogan passed during the credit titles were all emblems of aspects of his character. Lean, tough, unshaven, Hogan was a laconic gunman, a hard-bitten, dry-humoured loner, with nerves of steel and an endless supply of cheroots.

The film proper began with Hogan rescuing a semi-naked woman from three drunks who were trying to rape her. It was a big surprise when the woman put on her clothes and she turned out to be a nun. Not that this stopped Hogan flirting with her: 'I sure wish you weren't a nun . . . Maybe a nun ought not to be so good-looking . . . I sure would have liked to have met up with you before you took to them clothes and them vows.' But, randy though he was, he was a good boy and behaved himself.

Shirley MacLaine and Clint Eastwood in *Two Mules for Sister Sara*

There were many clues early on that Sister Sara was not a nun: she smoked a cigar, she swigged whiskey, she extracted a cork from a bottle with her teeth and her behaviour and language were rarely nun-like. 'Sober up, you dirty bastard, or I'll kill you!' she yelled, socking him on the jaw. It might have been better for the story if the clues had been more subtle and delayed until at least that moment when a dying French officer, to whom she was giving the last rites, recognized her and sat up on his deathbed, screaming, '*C'est toi!* You filthy bitch!' Sara dismissed it as delirium. If Boetticher had had his way, nobody would have known she was a prostitute until the end of the picture.

It would have been better, too, if Sara had made suckers of cinemagoers as well as Hogan, though it is very doubtful that regular cinema-

goers would ever have believed in Shirley MacLaine as a nun. MacLaine had made a career out of playing whores with hearts of gold in such films as *Some Came Running*, *Irma La Douce* and *Sweet Charity*. The role had, originally, been intended for Elizabeth Taylor. It is doubtful that many people would have believed in Taylor as a nun, either.

Sara, as became the most popular whore in the best whorehouse in Chihuahua, was a tough cookie, capable of frightening off the Yaqui Indians merely by brandishing her cross in their faces and dazzling them with its shiny surface. She was also capable of clambering up the trestle of a bridge, high over a gorge, to plant dynamite to blow up a supply train, and this despite having just said she had no head for heights. Siegel's favourite scene was the one where she removed an arrow protruding from Hogan's left shoulder after he had been wounded by the Yaquis. She had to cut a shaft in the arrow, fill it with gunpowder and then, when he ignited the powder, she had to knock the arrow right through his body with a sharp crack. If she didn't hit straight, the arrow would break inside him.

Sara wasn't just a sexual animal; she was also a political animal, helping the Juáristas (the Mexican guerrillas) in their revolution against the French. Unlike Hogan, she was not in it just for the money. When he discovered she was a whore (being the last person to do so, having, strangely, not noticed her eyebrows and mascara), he was initially furious, but, quickly making up for lost time, he barged into her bathroom. 'Come back later,' she said. 'I want to be all dressed up for you.' 'Who in the hell wants to see you dressed?' he asked, getting

into the bath with her, fully clothed. 'The least you can do is take off your hat,' she said. 'Haven't got time for that,' he replied, taking the cigar out of her mouth and sinking into the soap suds.

Siegel handled the comedy and the violence with equal skill. The climax, a raid on a French garrison, was carried out with characteristic vigour, realism and excitement. Tautly photographed, there were vivid scenes of destruction and death, including some horrific close-ups. The Juáristas were mown down by machine-gun bullets. The French were cut down by machetes. The staccato montage looked as if it had been lifted from the murals of Diego Rivera. Eastwood, meanwhile, nonchalantly lobbed dynamite, while smoking his cheroot.

Don Siegel directs Clint Eastwood in *Two Mules for Sister Sara*

Clint Eastwood in *Two Mules for Sister Sara*

Clint Eastwood in *Two Mules for Sister Sara*

The final scene had Sara and Hogan riding off to San Francisco with numerous hatboxes. She was dressed in gaudy scarlet, every inch the tart. Clearly, she was going to be an invaluable asset in his saloon. Just in case cinemagoers still had not appreciated the pun in the title, the shot made it clear that Hogan, her stubborn and reluctant aide, whom she had manipulated, cajoled and bullied throughout the picture, was the second mule.

Ennio Morricone's score maintained the tension and, as always, used church music with irony and wit. The Mexican locations, with their sweeping panoramas and brutal countryside, were superbly photographed by Gabriel Figueroa.

Clint Eastwood is the cowboy and Shirley MacLaine is the nun. Things might have been more entertaining if the roles had been reversed.

Derek Malcolm, *Guardian*

***Two Mules for Sister Sara* is a solidly entertaining film that provides Clint Eastwood with his best, most substantial role to date; in it he is far better than he has ever been. In director Don Siegel, Eastwood has found what John Wayne found in John Ford and Gary Cooper found in Frank Capra.**

Los Angeles Herald-Examiner

Eastwood looks grizzled, stares into the sun and sneers, but anything more demanding seems beyond his grasp.

Time

Clint Eastwood smoulders his way through a panierful of cigars.

G. Millar, *Listener*

The 1970s

KELLY'S HEROES

Directed by Brian G. Hutton   1970

We hope the laughs will come as thick as the bullets. The violence is de-personalized in the pop style of a comic book.

Brian G. Hutton

Kelly's Heroes came out the same year as *M*A*S*H* and *Catch-22* and treated World War II in the same flippant, ribald and cynical manner. Fourteen thousand bars of gold worth $16 million were in a bank 30 miles behind enemy lines, just waiting to be picked up. Twenty-seven GIs went absent without leave during their rest and recreation period. They set out to rob a bank and damn near won a war instead. If they'd got to be killed, they argued, they might just as well be killed risking their lives for themselves. Originally, there were going to be 30 GIs, but three characters were deliberately cut from the script so nobody would be able to tag the film 'The Dirty Thirty'. On set, the movie was known as 'The Clean Dozen'.

Kelly's heroes were not heroes; they were lechers, black marketeers, thieves and cowards. When they questioned prisoners, they weren't interested in military information; they wanted only to find out where the girls, hotels and restaurants were. 'You've got to think of us as tourists,' said the interrogating sergeant. The officers hadn't a clue what was going on. The army was run by men like Private Kelly, a former lieutenant who had been busted as a scapegoat for somebody else's error. Kelly was played by Clint Eastwood, cool, reliable, resourceful. There was never any doubt that he was the man in charge.

The action was very noisy. Everybody shouted. Everybody went way over the top.

Eastwood didn't. He left the 'acting' to Telly Savalas, Don Rickles, Carroll O'Connor and Donald Sutherland. He was the straight man; they were the comedians. Savalas was the bald, fatherly sergeant. Rickles was the enterprising, hustling, ever-complaining quartermaster. O'Connor was the bombastic, farcical general who dished out medals to the looters and was mistaken by the French for General de Gaulle.

The actor who ran away with all the reviews was Donald Sutherland, playing Oddball, a drugged-up-to-the-eyeballs, bearded hippie, totally freaked-out and given to saying things like, 'Don't hit me with the negatives so early in the morning.' What this pot-puffing, half-asleep, 1970s' dropout was doing in 1945 post D-Day France was anybody's guess.

Oddball was involved in the production's most unforgettable sequence, when his tank blasted its way through a railway goods yard to the sound of Hank Williams singing 'Sunshine', playing from its loudspeaker. (Twenty years later Francis Ford Coppola's helicopters in *Apocalypse Now* would go on a bombing raid with their loudspeakers blaring Wagner.) 'Sunshine' was a pleasant tune for cinemagoers to listen to while they were watching the enemy being massacred and buildings being blown up. Music was used satirically throughout; the ever-popular 'Burning Bridges', sung by The Mike Curb Congregation during the credit titles, was reprised twice.

Kelly's Heroes was an excuse for unlimited violence and mass killings. As he had proved in *Where Eagles Dare*, Brian Hutton was very adept at deploying vast numbers and he stage-managed the carnage and destruction with considerable flair. The film was shot in

Yugoslavia, the Yugoslavian government having allowed MGM not only to use their army but also to destroy the petite seventeenth-century town of Vizinada on the Istrian peninsula.

There was something obscene about the way the camera could watch any number of Germans being killed for the public's so-called entertainment, yet the moment two Americans were shot the soundtrack immediately went all plaintive and audiences were asked to take their deaths seriously. By the end of the picture there was hardly a German left alive, yet only three Americans had been killed and one wounded.

A confrontation between three American GIs and a German tank in a deserted street was a parody of every Western showdown. There were close-ups of the men's faces, close-ups of their rifles, close-ups of their hands on holsters and close-ups of their feet marching down the street to a twanging guitar parodying Ennio Morricone's score for the *Dollars* trilogy. The tank guarded the bank. The Americans negotiated a deal with the tank commander. If he blew a hole in the door, he could share in the spoils. The Americans' argument was simple: 'Look, Max, you and us, we're just soldiers, right? We don't know what this war is all about. All we do is fight and die. For what? We don't get anything out of it.' Max blew down the door.

Donald Sutherland, Clint Eastwood and Telly Savalas in *Kelly's Heroes*

Clint Eastwood in
Kelly's Heroes

On the screen Clint Eastwood is a man who knows where he's going. He knows what he's after and he knows how to get it. In an age of uncertainty in the arts, politics and everything else, people enjoy watching a man like this in action. They don't want to see the anguish of a Brando or a James Dean any more. They want to escape into something more positive.

Brian Hutton

Eastwood's performance remains in his traditional low-key groove, thereby creating an adrenalin vacuum filled to the brim by the screen-dominating presence of Savalas and Sutherland.

Variety

Clint Eastwood in
Kelly's Heroes

Clint Eastwood, who is not generally a funny man, plays with a quiet, thin-lipped determination of such withdrawn ferocity – as if he was a kind of

Gary Cooper whose essence had not just preceded but utterly superseded his existence – that you would expect his goal to be murder rather than money.

Roger Greenspun, *New York Times*

Eastwood manages not to change expressions once during the 146 minutes of this nonsense.

Judith Crist, *New York Magazine*

The film could have been one of the best war movies ever. And it should have been; it had the best script, a good cast, a subtle anti-war message. But somehow everything got lost. The picture got bogged down shooting in Yugoslavia and it just ended up as the story of a bunch of American screw-offs in World War II.

Clint Eastwood

THE BEGUILED

Directed by Don Siegel   1970

The Beguiled, a superb, stagey melodrama, was given the full-blown Southern baroque treatment by Don Siegel. The time was towards the end of the American Civil War, which was economically established during the credit titles by a black and white montage of Matthew Brady photographs. As the credit titles finished, colour seeped into the frame.

The setting was an elegant, delapidated, colonial mansion in a desolate Louisiana wasteland. The mansion was a seminary for young ladies, where the two teachers and their six charges lived in daily fear of being raped by both armies. They took a wounded Union soldier, with a broken leg, into the school and nursed him back to health.

Since there was no other man in the house, Corporal John McBurney (called McB), a sexual philanderer and opportunist, seized the moment. Clint Eastwood, at first bedridden and in his nightshirt and then hobbling about on crutches, was a manly, handsome, sexy rooster among gullible hens. He had plenty of seductive Yankee charm and gallantry. He was also a liar, pretending to be a pacifist and a Quaker when he was neither, his statements instantly belied by flashbacks on the screen.

'I am nobody's slave,' he declared; but he was, his captivity symbolized by a black crow with a broken wing, tied up on the porch. The women kept him prisoner and he offered them his services, partly to serve himself and partly because he didn't want them to hand him over. Siegel's taut direction maintained the tension throughout as to whether they would betray him or not.

The frustrated women, eavesdropping on each other, quickly made fools of themselves.

Mae Mercer, Jo Ann Harris, Geraldine Page, Clint Eastwood and Pamelyn Ferdin in *The Beguiled*

McB confessed he wasn't keen to have his head on the chopping block but, unable to deny his sexual urges, he abused his hospitality, flirted with them all, playing them off each other, and paid an exceptionally heavy price.

Geraldine Page was excellent as the strong-minded headmistress, Miss Martha, who had made love with her brother and who also, given half the chance, looked as if she might make love with her 22-year-old assistant, Miss Edwina, a former pupil. 'If this war goes on much longer,' she observed, 'I shall forget I was a woman.' Initially, she had intended to hand McB over, it being treason not to do so, but she changed her mind and invited him to stay. ('The place needs a man,' she argued.) She fantasized in front of a *pietà* by Van der Weyden, dreaming she and Edwina were in bed with McB and that McB was Christ and they were taking him down from the cross.

Elizabeth Hartman was affecting as Miss Edwina, a timid, Pre-Raphaelite virgin. McB said she was a sleeping beauty waiting in a castle for a prince to wake her with a kiss and so, when she found McB in bed with 17-year-old Carol, she threw him downstairs, breaking his leg. 'You lying bastard! You filthy lecher! I hope you're dead!'

Miss Martha (who had been expecting him to come to her room) exacted a terrible revenge. There was a memorably gruesome scene when, in order to save him from gangrene (so she said), she cut off his leg below the knee with a saw. He looked like a crucified figure, tied down on the dining table, and the sound of the saw was horrific.

'You dirty bitch!' he raged when he woke up and discovered what she had done. 'Just

68

Mae Mercer, Geraldine
Page and Clint Eastwood
in *The Beguiled*

because I didn't go to your bed, because I went to somebody else's bed . . . Why in the hell didn't you castrate me?' He turned nasty. He tried to blackmail Miss Martha, having stolen her love letters to her brother; he threatened to rape the black servant; and he killed Amy's pet turtle. Later, he apologized for his actions, saying he had been drunk, and announced his engagement to Miss Edwina at the dinner table, at the very moment he was eating the poisonous mushrooms which had been specially picked for him by Amy.

The actresses gave highly strung performances, in keeping with the theatrics, yet at the same time kept themselves tightly reined in, never descending to crude melodrama. Pamelyn Ferdin was 12-year-old Amy ('old enough for kisses,' said McB), who idolized him and believed he loved her. Jo Ann Harris was Carol, hussy and blackmailer, who encouraged McB's advances ('I bet there's not a soft spot on you'). Mae Mercer was the servant, who had been raped by Miss Edwina's brother. Of all the characters, she came across as the most modern, the only anachronism.

The Beguiled had a marvellous feeling for period and place. The darkened corridors, the rich furniture and the shuttered rooms provided an ideal setting for the claustrophobia and hysteria. Bruce Surtees's atmospheric camerawork was exceptionally fine. The production had a strange dream-like quality, the action regularly punctuated by flashbacks of reveries and hallucinations. There was a particularly haunting moment, which managed to be both realistic and eerie, when a Confederate wagon full of wounded and dying Yankees passed by the plantation.

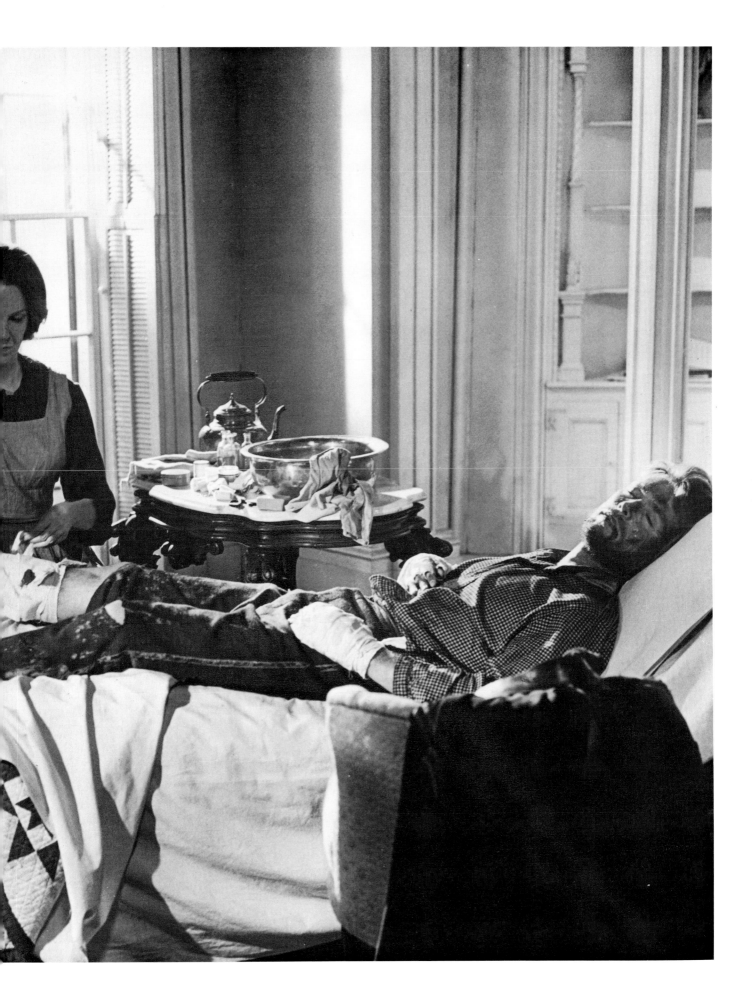

Elizabeth Hartman and
Clint Eastwood in
The Beguiled

At the end of the film, with McB's death, the colour seeped out of the frame, in the same way that it had seeped in.

Don Siegel directs this ironic, lethal story with a nice feeling for the grisly.

Dilys Powell, Sunday Times

Eastwood, working with Siegel for the third time, exudes cool, threatening sexuality.

Time

He seems only to exist that the sexual repressions of the women who surround him can find their ultimate expression. In consequence the movie takes on a misogynistic tone which a stronger actor would have countered. Eastwood's McBurney is strictly one-dimensional.

Andrew Tudor, New Society

The whole thing is managed with great address, well-paced, with atmospheres and undertones vividly and economically suggested, and a balance held adroitly between horror and *grand guignol* scepticism.

David Robinson, Financial Times

The family that likes to vomit together can do it at the movies . . . A must for sadists and woman-haters.

Judith Crist, New York Magazine

PLAY MISTY FOR ME

Directed by Clint Eastwood   1971

Play Misty For Me, an updated *film noir*, paid homage to the psychological thrillers of the 1940s and borrowed freely from Alfred Hitchcock, Roman Polanski and Claude Chabrol.

The camera flew in to Carmel and the Monterey peninsula. Clint Eastwood was cast as Dave Garver, a popular, late-night Californian disc jockey on a local radio station who offered 'a little verse, a little talk and five hours of music to be very, very nice to each other by'. One of his regular fans, who kept asking him to play Errol Garner's 'Misty', picked him up at a bar (where Don Siegel, making his acting debut, was the bartender).

At first Evelyn was merely an embarrassing nuisance who refused to be rejected after a one-night stand. 'There are no strings,' she agreed, 'but I never said anything about not coming back for seconds.' The story became every man's nightmare. Dave found he had a neurotic and persistent sexual blackmailer on his hands, pathologically possessive, impossibly demanding. 'Why are you pretending you don't love me?' she screamed. 'We don't even know each other!' he retorted.

The suicidal intensity was carefully charted. Jessica Walter, eager and edgy, sweet and savage, sexy and predatory, acted with frightening believability, redefining a woman scorned. There were plenty of fireworks, sudden, unnerving bursts of temper and incredible rudeness towards strangers, neighbours and, on one memorable occasion, towards a woman producer who was having a business lunch with Dave.

Eastwood played a surprisingly passive victim. Why didn't he go to the police? (Had he

Clint Eastwood and Jessica Walter in *Play Misty for Me*

done so, there would, of course, have been no film.) Dave may have looked a nice guy, but he was essentially dishonest, a not very bright womanizer, thoughtless, selfish, sleeping around, quick to take advantage and not wanting any emotional involvement. The strength of Eastwood's performance was its honesty; he did not hide what Dave was.

The mood of terror was sustained throughout. Evelyn became a homicidal maniac, wielding scissors and carving knives, destroying his home and attempting to murder his housekeeper and his girlfriend. Particularly effective was the scene when he was asleep, having a nightmare that Evelyn was in his bedroom with a knife, only to find that he was awake, that he wasn't having a nightmare and it was for real.

Clint Eastwood and
Jessica Walter in
Play Misty for Me

There was a long lyrical sequence in the
forest with his former long-time lover, who had
abandoned him because of his promiscuity.
They kissed, they bathed, they made love.
There was even a red sunset. It all looked like
an advertisement for the song 'The First Time
Ever I Saw Your Face,' sung by Roberta Flack,
which went straight into the charts. The
lovemaking gave way to the Monterey Jazz
Festival, to which Eastwood took a documentary rather than a dramatic approach. These
two intervals, deliberate respites from the
violence, went on far too long.

The end degenerated into melodrama, the
camera constantly cutting from Evelyn slashing
away at a painting to Dave in his car (a cavalry
of one) driving to the rescue. Arriving at the
house, which was, naturally, plunged in darkness, he bent over the tied-up body of his girlfriend, only to have Evelyn strike his shoulder,
his arm, his chest and his leg. Despite his

Clint Eastwood and
Don Siegel in
Play Misty for Me

wounds, he managed to summon up enough
strength for the final *coup de grâce*, a punch to
the jaw which sent her reeling over the balcony
and on to the cliffs below. The climax,
depending upon your point of view, was either
parody of the genre or sheer banality.

Brad Whitney of Carmel got a credit for
Eastwood's wardrobe and at times it did seem
that he was modelling clothes and underwear
for them.

**Clint Eastwood's *Play Misty for Me* is a doubly
encouraging directorial debut, successful both as a
controlled and original psychological thriller and as
a stylish *homage* to Eastwood's cinematic mentor,
Don Siegel.**

Nigel Andrews, *Monthly Film Bulletin*

**Eastwood displays a vigorous talent for sequences of
violence and tension. He has obviously seen *Psycho*
and *Repulsion* more than once, but these are
excellent texts and he has learned his lesson passing
well.**

Jay Cocks, *Time*

**A performance even more understated than usual.
He doesn't rise to such parts but allows himself to
lapse into them.**

Andrew Tudor, *New Society*

**The film is grotesque, narcissistic (Eastwood in his
underpants), but without sparkle. The actor being
transparency itself, it was difficult for him to have a
presence. A real zombie.**

M. G., *Cinéma*

DIRTY HARRY

Directed by Don Siegel   1971

*It's not about a man who stands for violence,
it's about a man who can't understand society
tolerating violence.*

Clint Eastwood

Dirty Harry, a vicious urban thriller, began with
a shot of a memorial plaque paying tribute to
the police officers of San Francisco who had
given their lives in the line of duty.

Scorpio, a rooftop sniper, was holding the
city to ransom, promising to kill one person
every day unless he was paid $100,000. Girls,
priests and blacks were to be his targets. The
story was based on the crimes of the notorious
real-life Zodiac killer.

Detective Harry Callahan (called Dirty Harry,
because he was willing to do every dirty job
that came along) was given the job of delivering the ransom money. He had to follow a
series of instructions. Scorpio (who wore a belt
with a peace sign, giving much offence in some
quarters) gave Harry the runaround, bouncing
him all over town, from phone booth to phone
booth, allowing him barely any time at all to
get from Point A to Point B and threatening all
the time to kill a girl he had taken hostage. The
girl was, in fact, already raped and dead. Later
there was a gritty, stark documentary shot of
her naked body being lifted out of a manhole.

The destination was the huge cross at Mount
Davidson Park, a good place to get mugged,
picked up by a male prostitute and beaten to a
pulp by a serial killer wearing a mask. An even
better location was the floodlit Kezar Stadium,
where he ran Scorpio to ground. Scorpio
whined, blubbed and pleaded hysterically with
Callahan not to shoot him, insisting on his
rights. There were huge close-ups of his

Andy Robinson
and Clint Eastwood
in *Dirty Harry*

77

frightened face. Callahan was unflinching in his brutality. The last shot was breathtaking, starting with a close-up of him trampling on Scorpio's gaping wound and the camera pulling back and back until the two tiny figures disappeared in the darkness.

Scorpio (a memorable creation by Andy Robinson, son of Edward G.) was not brought to trial because Callahan had denied him medical attention and his legal rights to a counsel. The mayor gave his word that the criminal would not be molested. Harry, who was always much more interested in the rights of the victim than those of the criminal, was bitingly sarcastic ('I'm all broken up about this man's rights') and when Scorpio was released, he continued to harass him. The pursuit became an obsession.

Callahan never bothered to disguise his contempt for his superiors. When he was asked what proof he had that a man he had shot was going to rape a woman, he replied: 'When a naked man is chasing a woman through an alley with a butcher's knife and a hard-on, I figure he isn't out collecting for the Red Cross.' What informed Eastwood's performance was Harry's deep anger, his cold hatred and bitter resentfulness about the sacrifices the public and the cop on the street were expected to make. His fight was as much with the legal and political system that could not protect its citizens properly and stopped him doing his job.

Scorpio hijacked a busload of schoolchildren and threatened to shoot them if he wasn't paid $200,000 and provided with a jet to make his getaway. The major agreed. 'Nothing cute, nothing fancy,' said Callahan's immediate boss,

'just pay the ransom and report back here.' Harry had other ideas. There was a great shot of him waiting on a bridge which ran over the highway. He stood there like some mythical figure out of a Western, ready to leap on top of the bus. (Eastwood did his own stunt.) There followed a manic, gibbering ride, the bus swerving from side to side, as Scorpio tried to throw him off.

The building yard of a quarry company provided the setting for the final chase and shoot-out. Scorpio was cornered and took a little boy hostage, using him as a shield. Harry had a speech he had already used earlier in the film and which has passed into movie folklore: 'I know what you are thinking, punk. You're thinking did he fire six shots or only five. Now to tell you the truth I have forgotten. But being as this is a .44 magnum, the most powerful handgun in the world that will blow your head clean off, you'd have to ask yourself a question. Do I feel lucky? Well, do you, punk?' Scorpio ended up dead in the water. To nail a bastard, you needed a bastard.

Don Siegel, master of narrative, directed at a cracking pace and there was plenty of suspense. Good use was made of San Francisco, its streets, alleys, rooftops, freeways and industrial suburbs. A neon sign (Jesus Saves), lit up at night, dominated the skyline, making a nice, ironic comment. There was an excellent, eerie score by Lalo Schifrin.

The very last shot had Callahan throwing his badge away, just like Gary Cooper had done in *High Noon*. The box office, however, insisted he retrieve it, and he went on to make four more 'Dirty Harry' films: *Magnum Force*, *The Enforcer*, *Sudden Impact* and *The Dead Pool*.

Eastwood gives his best performance so far – tense, full of implicit identification with his character.

Jay Cocks, *Time*

If he had used a better lead than Clint Eastwood, who is really more of a blessing to a lighting cameraman than to a director, he would have made a film to remember.

Christopher Hudson, *Spectator*

With policemen like Clint Eastwood and cowboys like John Wayne civilization has nothing to fear.

Ian Christie, *Daily Express*

His message has the disconcerting tone of someone calling out the vigilantes.

Playboy

Dirty Harry is obviously just a genre movie, but this action genre has always had fascist potential, and it has finally surfaced . . . since crime is caused by deprivation, misery, psychopathology and social injustice, *Dirty Harry* is a deeply immoral movie.

Pauline Kael, *New Yorker*

We were only interested in making the film a successful one, both as entertainment and at the box office. I can't understand why, when a film is made purely for entertainment, it should be criticized on a political basis.

Don Siegel

Clint Eastwood in
Dirty Harry

JOE KIDD

Directed by John Sturges   1972

A guy sits in the audience; he's 25 and scared stiff about what he's going to do with his life. He wants to be that self-sufficient thing he sees up there on the screen in my pictures. A super-human character who has all the answers, is doubly cool, exists on his own without society or the help of society's police forces.

Clint Eastwood

The time was the turn of the century, the place was New Mexico and the subject was ethnic minority rights and social injustice. The Mexican Americans were being cheated by grasping American landowners, who were in connivance with the legal system to gain control of their land. Trying to press their rights in the courtroom of the small town of Sinola, they were given the runaround by a prejudiced judge.

Luis Chama (John Saxon), the Mexican revolutionary leader, gave a public demonstration of his anger when he burned the courtroom records and attempted to kidnap the judge. He was foiled by Joe Kidd (Clint Eastwood), who happened to be in the courtroom at the time, having been arrested the night before for poaching, being disorderly and avoiding arrest.

Joe, who had killed a deer on a reservation and threatened to urinate over the courthouse, preferred to stay in jail for 10 days rather than pay a $10 fine. Frank Harlan (Robert Duvall), one of the grasping landowners, paid the fine and hired Joe to track down Chama. Initially, dressed like a town dude, Joe looked cute in his derby and cut a sexy figure. He flirted openly with Harlan's mistress, even while one of Harlan's men was looking on, and, strange to

John Saxon, Ron Sable, Stella Garcia and Clint Eastwood in *Joe Kidd*

say, the man didn't bother to report the incident to his boss.

Eastwood, cast in his familiar role of impassive, fearless gunfighter, acted with his familiar laconic, laid-back charm and movie-goers could sit back, safe in the knowledge that if Joe were captured, he would escape and kill any number of bad guys single-handed. The performance was low-key and casual. The violence was all bottled up, except in the opening scene when, bruised and hungover, he threw his coffee over his jailer's face and bashed him in the face with a saucepan.

Harlan wasn't the sort of man who was going to waste time arguing his non-existent case in court. You could tell he was the really bad guy by the fancy way he dressed and the manner in which he addressed the Mexicans. 'We can cut off your ears,' he said to one poor chap. 'We can cut off something else, too,' added one of his gang. Harlan had a nasty habit of killing people in cold blood. However, it was when he threatened to shoot innocent villagers in batches of five that Joe, already equivocal in his loyalties, began to realize he had made a mistake in working for him and switched sides.

The screenplay was by Elmore Leonard, author of *Hombre*, one of the best Westerns of the 1960s. The story was meant to trace Joe's journey towards moral understanding, but Joe's motives remained obscure and the trans-formation of his character never happened, basically because there was no character to transform.

Everybody was unscrupulous. Chama was willing to sacrifice a whole village rather than give himself up. 'We only win if I stay alive,' he declared. So it was very unconvincing when

Joe persuaded him to return to Sinola and to allow justice to take its course, especially since Chama had first-hand experience of American justice.

Don Stroud (who had played the murderer in *Coogan's Bluff*) was cast as Lamarr, one of Harlan's gang, and he had a rough time at the hands of Joe, being pushed down the stairs and hit in the face with the butt of a rifle. The only reason he didn't shoot Joe in the back (and he had plenty of opportunities to do so) was because the hero doesn't get killed half-way through a movie. It is the ugly bad guys, like Lamarr, who get killed off.

If the set looked a bit flimsy and ready for demolition, it became clear why this was so when Joe commandeered a steam train and drove through the buffers and into the town, ending up in the saloon. 'Got a prisoner for you!' he yelled. 'Jesus, Joe!' said the bartender, giving him a rifle. The steam train got the best notices.

The final shoot-out took place in the courtroom, where Joe, symbolically sitting in the judge's chair and acting as judge, jury and executioner, shot Harlan down and ordered the weak and compromised sheriff (Gregory Walcott) out of the courtroom. There was a wonderful close-up of Eastwood's searing eyes blazing with anger right across the screen's wide, letter-box frame. 'Is there anything I can do for you, Joe?' asked the sheriff. Joe replied with a very predictable punch to the jaw.

Clint Eastwood in
Joe Kidd

Clint Eastwood in
Joe Kidd

Clint Eastwood is one of the very few new stars who work absolutely in the old way. He is not exactly the most varied of actors; but just as a presence he holds the screen with total conviction: you can safely drape a film around him and be sure it will not crumple to the floor in a shapeless tangle.

John Russell Taylor, *The Times*

The casual authority with which Eastwood wields a shotgun while chucking down sandwiches and beer convinces us that John Wayne's mantle as Avenging Conscience of the Right will not go unclaimed after the Duke's passing.

Michael McKegney, *Village Voice*

The film's sympathies are all in the right liberal place; but it's tiresomely discursive and listless about its story-telling.

David Robinson, *Financial Times*

HIGH PLAINS DRIFTER

Directed by Clint Eastwood   1972

High Plains Drifter *was great fun because I liked the irony of it. I liked the irony of doing a stylized version of what happens if the sheriff in* High Noon *is killed and symbolically comes back as some avenging angel – and I think that's more hip than doing just a straight Western, the straight old conflicts we've all seen.*

Clint Eastwood

For a publicity shot, Eastwood had stood on the set of the town's cemetery, leaning on two gravestones bearing the names of Sergio Leone and Don Siegel, an acknowledgement of his debt to them. Well-written and well-directed, *High Plains Drifter* was a highly imaginative revenge story, one of the best Westerns of the 1970s and probably the first ever supernatural Western. The emphasis was on the archetypal myth rather than believable action. The film's title was a pun.

The setting was Lago, a frontier town in America's south-west in 1870. A lone rider came out of a hazy landscape to a weird and spooky soundtrack. The music stopped and gave way to just the sound of his horse's hooves on the gravel. It was some time before his face was seen. He remained totally impassive until he heard the crack of a whip. Once he had dismounted, the only sound was the clinking of his spurs. The whole sequence, alternating between the Stranger and the townspeople observing him, was a skilful introduction, a leisurely star entrance, beautifully photographed and edited by Bruce Surtees and Ferris Webster respectively.

The Stranger, dirty, unshaven, softly-spoken, wearing a magnificent long coat and a wide-brimmed hat, entered the saloon and ordered a beer. 'Sleeping-range bums don't usually stop in Lago. Life is a little too quick for them,' he was advised by one of three louts standing at the bar. 'I'm faster than you'll ever live to be,' he murmured and shortly afterwards, to prove his point, he shot the three louts dead. 'What did you say your name was?' asked the barber.

A coarse and volatile whore (Mariana Hill), who called him 'trash' and then, ill-advisedly, accused him of not being a man, was dragged off to a stable and given 'a lesson in manners': i.e. she was raped in broad daylight. Nobody came to her rescue; only a dwarf came to gawp. She was so angry she shot him three times while he was taking a bath in a tub and smoking a cigar; he merely disappeared under the water to resurface, still smoking his cigar. He then went to the local hotel and lay down on his bed and dreamt of a terrible whipping. The nightmare (to a spooky accompaniment on the soundtrack) would recur, but the second time round the sequence would be seen through the memory of the dwarf.

The town hired the Stranger as a gunfighter to protect them from three returning troubleshooters who had been in jail for a year. They offered him a free hand and anything he wanted. Taking them at their word, he appointed the dwarf as mayor and sheriff and requisitioned weaponry, drink, food, wood, blankets and the hotel. He bossed, rooked and humiliated them all and soon they were at each other's throats. 'I knew you were cruel, but I didn't know how far you could go,' said the hotelier's wife (Verna Bloom). 'Well, you still don't,' he replied. Finally, he forced them to paint the whole town red, including the

church, and alter its name to Hell. It couldn't have been worse if the devil himself had ridden into Lago.

The Stranger, having trained them in the art of defence, deserted them at the very moment the troubleshooters were riding into town and he did not return until they had all been rounded up. He then dealt with the trio personally, whipping one to death, hanging another and shooting down the third. The killings were played out against the burning buildings, a flaming, hellish background. 'Who are you?' screamed Geoffrey Lewis in his role of leading troubleshooter.

The Stranger was Jim Duncan, their former sheriff, come back from beyond the grave to settle a private score and take his revenge, not only on his murderers but also on the citizens, who had stood by and let him be killed. The three troubleshooters were the men who had whipped him to death. (This had already been signalled on their first appearance, on their release from prison, when the soundtrack had played a variation on the spooky theme.) Eastwood, impassive, unearthly, totally without pity, was a charismatic spectre in black, a man to make people afraid, yet what was so good about the performance was the dry humour he brought to the role.

The fact that Buddy Van Horn was credited with playing the Marshal was misleading; perhaps deliberately so. Van Horn played the Marshal only in the sense that he was the stuntman who stood in for Eastwood in the scene where he was whipped to death. In the original script, the High Plains Drifter was Jim Duncan's brother; the credit allowed cinema-goers to think he still could be; and, of course,

Mariana Hill and
Clint Eastwood in
High Plains Drifter

if he were the brother, it might help to explain
why the people of Lago did not recognize him.

The supporting characters – the mine owners
(Mitchell Ryan and Jack Ging), the mayor
(Stefan Gierasch), the hotelier (Ted Hartley),
the sheriff (Walter Barnes), the barber (William
O'Connell), the preacher (Robert Donner) –
were all from stock but, within their one-
dimensional terms, they were well-observed
and Ernest Tidyman's cynical screenplay
mocked their 'short supply of guts' and their
farcical ineptitude with firearms. The dwarf
was played by Billy Curtis, who had played the
Lord High Mayor of the Munchkins in *The
Wizard of Oz*.

Eastwood's own performance and his
direction were badly underrated by the critics.
The production, shot in continuity, had a
dream-like quality, the bleak and desolate
countryside ideal for the surreal and allegorical
subject matter. Bruce Surtees's expressive

photography, with its low-key atmospheric
lighting and imaginative angling and framing of
individual shots, was superb.

**I suppose you could call it a supernatural Western
except that there is nothing natural about it and it
certainly isn't super.**

Ian Christie, *Daily Express*

**What emerges is a narcissistic essay in style, in
which characterization and story development are
too often sacrificed to the visual tricks and
mannerisms of Eastwood's camerawork.**

Nigel Andrews, *Financial Times*

**As a director, Clint Eastwood is not as good as he
seems to think he is. As an actor, he is probably
better than he allows himself to be . . . Rarely are
humble Westerns permitted to drift around on such
a highfalutin plain.**

Richard Schickel, *Time*

**As a pasta-parable it drowns in its own ketchup . . .
This is the kind of film that relies on the savage
shimmer of its visuals to blind us to its lack of ethic.**

Tom Hutchinson, *Sunday Telegraph*

**I can see the cineastes hovering over it like vultures
over the body of the West.**

Derek Malcolm, *Guardian*

**John Wayne didn't like *High Plains Drifter* and let
me know it. He wrote me a letter putting it down,
saying it was not the West. I was trying to get away
from what he and Gary Cooper and others had
done.**

Clint Eastwood quoted by Peter McDonald,
Evening Standard

BREEZY

Directed by Clint Eastwood   1973

Breezy was the name of a 17-year-old vagrant hippie (Kay Lenz), who was having a romantic affair with a 50-year-old divorced real estate salesman (William Holden). The affair was handled with sensitivity and quiet amusement by the scriptwriter, Jo Heims. The result was a matinée mixture of lyrical slush and sharp mordancy, with a subtle performance by Holden and an astringent one by Lenz.

It's performed beautifully, laced with a quietly ironic wit, and quite lovely to look at.

Geoff Andrew, *Time Out*

Unluckily, in the charmless performance and staging it emerges rather more simply as a middle-aged man's erotic nymphet daydream.

David Robinson, *The Times*

Fifty-year-old estate agents with a sentimental streak might enjoy it.

Ian Christie, *Daily Express*

Clint Eastwood and
William Holden on
the set of *Breezy*

MAGNUM FORCE

Directed by Ted Post   1973

Magnum Force began with a famous quote from *Dirty Harry*: 'This is a .44 magnum, the most powerful handgun in the world, and it could blow your head clean off. Do you feel lucky?' Both the line and the gun were aimed directly at the cinemagoer in the cinema. The poster had already made it abundantly clear that Harry Callahan's magnum was his phallus.

Once again the theme was law and order. Two hundred murders had been committed in the city during the previous year. A racket-eering trade union leader, who had been indicted for 23 of them and had not been convicted, had murdered a union reformer and got away with it yet again because of a legal technicality. While he was being driven from the courthouse along the highway, he, his attorney, his bodyguard and his driver were all shot at point-blank range by a cop on a motor-cycle. Something of a voyeur, the cop then went on to shoot naked gangsters in a swim-ming-pool and naked drug traffickers in bed, throwing one unlucky girl out of a window. 'Someone is trying to put the courts out of business,' observed Harry's boss. 'So far you've said nothing wrong,' replied Harry.

The cop, in his leather gear, boots and goggles, looked every inch a fascist and, since his face was hidden by the visor of his white crash helmet, every moviegoer who had seen *Dirty Harry* immediately jumped to the conclusion that Callahan was impersonating the cop, killing off all the top criminals in the city and saving the tax payer a lot of money. After all, it was well known that nobody hated hoodlums as much as he did and that he had never seen anything wrong in shooting people, so long as the right people got shot.

Hal Holbrook and
Clint Eastwood in
Magnum Force

90

Callahan discovered that the cop was actually one of four rookie cops and that there was a whole organization working within the police force (a sort of death squad on the Brazilian model) that was taking the law into its own hands, acting as judge, jury and freelance public executioners. Earlier, before he knew that they were the murderers, he had been impressed with their skill down at the shooting range. When his partner had told him about rumours going round that they were all homosexual, this hadn't worried Harry one bit: 'If the rest of you could shoot like them, I wouldn't care a damn if the whole department were queer!'

The rookies, who had obviously seen *Dirty Harry* and were clearly Callahan's disciples, managed to out-dirty Dirty Harry. The leader of the quartet (David Soul) argued that they were simply ridding society of killers who would be caught and sentenced anyway, if the courts worked properly. 'It's not just a question of whether or not to use violence. There's simply no other way.'

'I'm afraid you have misjudged me,' replied Harry, answering not only them but all his critics and making it unequivocal that he didn't approve of the vigilantes and that he upheld the law. 'I hate the goddamn system, but until someone comes along with some changes that make sense, I'll stick with it.'

Lieutenant Briggs (Hal Holbrook), his superior and a nasty bit of work, was in charge of the vigilantes. He tried to justify their actions by talking about retribution; the police, he said, had to use the same methods as the criminals if they were to win.

Magnum Force ended with *Bullitt*-like car and motorcycle chases and a facile climax in a deserted shipyard with Callahan and the rookies creeping around the hold of a ship, playing hide-and-seek. Harry was in fine fettle, knocking Briggs out, punching one rookie to death and then driving straight into another. And just when you thought the movie was over, Briggs was back and threatening to prosecute him for killing three cops. 'Who's going to believe you?' he cried, driving off. 'You're a killer, a maniac!' Seconds later his car blew up. 'A man's got to know his limitations,' observed Harry, who had planted the bomb.

In *Dirty Harry*, Callahan had been described as hating Limeys, Micks, Hebes, fat Dagos, Niggers, Hunkies, Chinks, Mexicans. Now, just in case anybody should have got the impression that he was a racist, his new partner was black (Felton Perry) and the girl downstairs (Adele Yoshioka) was Chinese. She asked him what she had to do to go to bed with him. This was a question many female cinemagoers had been asking themselves ever since the 'Dollars' trilogy. The answer was pretty encouraging. 'Try knocking on the door,' he said.

There was a terribly unconvincing sequence on a hijacked plane, when he was disguised as a pilot. It was there for a gratuitous shoot-out and a quick joke. 'This may sound silly, but can you fly?' asked his co-pilot as they drove down the runway. 'No, never had a lesson.' The incident belonged in another movie. A shoot-out in a shop was more relevant and far more exciting. There was a moment of real tension when a bomb had been delivered to his partner's letter box and he was desperately trying to phone and warn him.

Clint Eastwood in
Magnum Force

93

Clint Eastwood and
David Soul in
Magnum Force

Clint Eastwood re-creates the maverick cop with all
his charismatic if dubious magnetism.

George Melly, *Observer*

The trouble with right-wing films masquerading as
left-wing films attacking right-wing politics is that
they get into such embarrassing knots. How to
convince people that you are against chaps taking
the law into their own hands when your hero can
only survive by doing just that?

Gavin Millar, *Listener*

A cruel and largely humourless film, frenetically
directed by Ted Post, but irresistibly exciting even
when there is hardly a character for whom you give
a damn.

Cecil Wilson, *Daily Mail*

By turning Harry Callahan into a hypocrite, the
makers of *Magnum Force* expose their own
hypocrisy, as well as their lack of understanding of
the Eastwood phenomenon.

Jon Landau, *Rolling Stone*

The violence, as usual, offended a lot of
people. One criminal, making his getaway, had
a metal girder smash through the windscreen of
his car and right into his body. There was also
an unpleasant scene in the back of a taxi cab
when a black pimp (Albert Popwell) got his
orgasm while murdering a double-dealing
prostitute by pouring a can of drain cleaner
down her throat.

As for Eastwood, deadshot and deadpan, he
was his familiar dour, hard-bitten, cynical self.

Clint Eastwood isn't offensive; he isn't an actor, so
one could hardly call him a bad actor. He'd have to
do something before we could consider him bad at it
. . . Eastwood's inexpressiveness travels prepos-
terously well. He's utterly unbelievable in his
movies – inhumanely tranquil, controlled and
assured – and yet he seems to represent something
that isn't so unbelievable.

Pauline Kael, *New Yorker*

THUNDERBOLT AND LIGHTFOOT

Directed by Michael Cimino   1974

*The wolf shall dwell with the lamb and the
leopard shall lie down with the kid.*

Isaiah 11.6

Thunderbolt and Lightfoot, part buddy movie,
part chase movie, part bank robbery movie, a
story of greed and brutality, began as farce,
turned to thriller and ended in tragedy.
Michael Cimino's direction was taut and the
pace was fast. His screenplay had a genuine
freshness, with a real eye for character,
situation and detail. The locations in Montana
and round Great Falls, photographed by Frank
Stanley, were beautiful and provided a
wonderful backdrop.

The action got off to an arresting start when a
sermon in a small country church was interrupted by a man firing a gun. The preacher beat
a hasty retreat across the wheatfield (an
Andrew Wyeth landscape), hotly pursued by
the wheezing gunman. Shot in the arm, he was
saved by a young man who happened to be
driving past in a car he had just stolen.

The preacher (Clint Eastwood) was not really
a preacher, but a professional safe-breaker in
disguise, the notorious Thunderbolt, hunted by
his former partner-in-crime, Red Leary, who
believed, quite wrongly, that he had pocketed
half a million dollars from their last bank raid.
The money was, in fact, stashed behind a
blackboard in a nineteenth-century one-room
schoolhouse.

The amateur car thief (Jeff Bridges) was
called Lightfoot, a charming, talkative, self-
confident and not very bright 23-year-old
drifter, with a big grin and a cliché ready for
every occasion. They made a good pair, the
camaraderie nicely developed, the age

Jeff Bridges and Clint
Eastwood in *Thunderbolt
and Lightfoot*

difference and clash of personalities working
very much in the script's favour. Bridges, brash
and breezy, provided the exuberance.
Eastwood, jaded and grainy, provided the
restraint. The rapport between the two actors
was self-evident.

George Kennedy played the brutal, asthmatic
Red Leary. Geoffrey Lewis played Goody, his
weak-kidneyed partner who was always getting
in the way and seemed never to know what to
do in an emergency. 'WHAT DO YOU WANT ME TO
DO, RED? ('Kill the son of a bitch!') 'HERE?'
('Yes.') 'NOW?' ('Now.') Lewis and Kennedy
made a comic duo, especially when they were
driving around, squashed together in a silly
ice-cream van; except there was nothing funny
about the way Leary kicked Goody out of the
car when Goody was shot and left him to die in
the road. Leary himself came to a sadistic end,
savaged (off-screen) by a guard dog.

There was no consistency of tone and the
appeal of the film lay in the way Cimino mixed
light-hearted humour and freewheeling
violence. The screenplay was often extremely
funny in its small touches, as, for instance, in
an incident when a girl, wearing only her
panties and bra, ran out of a chalet, crying
'Rape!' 'Do you think we should stop here?'
asked a horrified woman, driving up in a car.
'Why not?' asked her husband. Thunderbolt
had just had sex with the girl; or rather, she
had just had sex with him and he hadn't
enjoyed the experience one bit. The leopard
would probably have preferred to have lain
down with the kid; the gay subtext was always
there for those who wanted it.

There was, too, an amusing scene when a
bank manager and his wife were tied up and so
were their daughter and the daughter's boy-
friend, who happened to be in her bed at the
time. The robbers, having put pingpong balls in
their mouths, left the couple as naked as they
had found them and put everything back in
place, only reversing their positions so that the
boy was now underneath the girl.

There were some nice jokes, in passing,
about the use of credit cards and feminists, on
motorbikes, wielding hammers against male
chauvinist motorists. There was also a farcical
cameo performance by Bill McKinney as a
crazy driver, a real nutter, travelling with a
boot full of rabbits so he could let them loose

and shoot them. Cliff Emmich was perfectly cast as a fat security man, whiling away the time reading pornography and seduced by Lightfoot disguised as a flirtatious girl. Bridges in drag remained resolutely masculine and parked his gun in the back of his underpants.

The film ended with Thunderbolt buying Lightfoot his dream car, a white Cadillac. Lightfoot died before he could use it. The unexpected, downbeat finish was highly affecting; all the more so for audiences not having fully appreciated just how severely hurt Lightfoot had been after a vicious beating by Leary. 'We made it,' he said just before he died. 'Do you know something? I felt us accomplished something, a good job. I feel proud of myself, like a hero.' Thunderbolt's loss was palpable.

Eastwood, always an unselfish actor, let Bridges run away with the film and Bridges, easy, relaxed and clearly enjoying himself, was immensely likeable. He got all the notices and was nominated for an Oscar. He had already been nominated for an Oscar at 21 for his performance in *The Last Picture Show*.

Mr Eastwood grows more appealing with every movie.

John Coleman, *New Statesman*

A film that grips the heart without insulting the intellect.

Tom Hutchinson, *Sunday Telegraph*

Eastwood unwinds a little from his customary characterization of a terse, razor-eyed stranger, breaking through to a kind boyish affability . . .

Jay Cocks, *Time*

Clint Eastwood and Jeff Bridges in *Thunderbolt and Lightfoot*

Eastwood remains Eastwood even when he is showing, in effect, the obverse side of Dirty Harry.

Hugh Herbert, *Guardian*

They [the public] prefer the seemingly ordinary fellow who speaks in a voice and idiom they can understand. They identify with him when he merely shrugs his shoulders in disbelief at the inanity that passes across the screen. And they feel for him when he lashes out against it – after society has intruded on his freedom and sense of order. Above all, they admire his street smarts.

Jon Landau, *Rolling Stone*

THE EIGER SANCTION

Directed by Clint Eastwood   1975

The Eiger is a mountain in Switzerland. Sanction was a codename for a killing. The Eiger is grim, observed somebody. So was the film.

Clint Eastwood was cast as an art historian lecturing on art in an American college. He was a former climber who had failed to climb the Eiger twice. ('He could climb all over me,' confessed one of his female students to a girlfriend.) He was also a retired assassin – codename Hemlock – tempted back into service by the promise of $20,000 and a painting by Pissarro. He already had a large and clandestine collection of Impressionists, 21 masterpieces by such artists as El Greco, Matisse and Klee, all bought with the fees from his killings.

Hemlock, without conscience and motivated only by greed and avarice, was liable to throw his assailants out of windows and beat up their bodyguards. He wore dark glasses and was willing to scale drainpipes and even mountains to get his man. He agreed to a sanction if he was given an Internal Revenue statement saying that he was the legal owner of the art collection and without tax liability. 'You drive a hard bargain,' observed Dragon, the head of a spy network, a total albino, who could not stand either light, cold or germs and whose blood needed to be changed every six months. The cartoon-like Dragon, a bulbous, blind freak whose scenes were filmed in a blood-red glow, was just the sort of silly character you would normally expect to find in a James Bond movie.

Hemlock's major target was one of a number of international climbers on the north face of the Eiger. The question was, which one? Dragon didn't know. Hemlock went into

training, limbering up in Mountain Valley, Arizona, a familiar and much-loved location, home of stagecoaches, wagons, Injuns, the US cavalry and John Wayne. 'How old are you? 35?' asked his trainer. 'Give or take,' replied Eastwood with a wry smile, looking as rugged and as weathered as the Eiger. George Kennedy played the trainer, an old buddy, a loud, jovial, hail-fellow-well-met type.

Hemlock practised on the 600-foot needle rock, which the Indians called The Totem, and very phallic it looked, too. There was a staggering helicopter shot to prove that Eastwood and Kennedy had actually been on top of the peak. They were there for five hours while the camera crew got the right shots. 'I defy anyone,' said Clint Eastwood in an interview with Victor David of the *Daily Express*, 'to watch it and not get that lurching feeling that we are in real danger up there. The trick was a hair-raising one to pull off successfully but every time I hear someone say "Wow" I feel happy. However, I don't think I'll be trying anything like it again. The helicopter actually lowered us on to the top, which is criss-crossed with cracks so that you think the whole structure is about to disintegrate.'

One of Hemlock's sanctions was a gay, Miles (Jack Cassidy), who was so gay that he had a dog called Faggot. Hemlock drove Miles far into the desert and abandoned him without food and water. Faggot decided to ditch his mistress and hitched a lift back in Hemlock's car.

Hemlock, who had quite a reputation as a stud, had sex only twice during the whole course of the film and on both occasions it was with unfortunate results. The first time he was

Clint Eastwood and the professional climbers/ cameramen on top of The Totem in Mountain Valley in *The Eiger Sanction*

together. The spy story got lost on the mountains. Audiences, who should have been wondering who the killer was, were just watching climbers, played by bad actors. Eastwood's direction was fatally slack and the climbing failed to excite.

The score tried very hard (too hard) to make drama where there was none. The basic trouble was that the whole cinema knew that George Kennedy was playing the villain. The only person who didn't know was Hemlock; and he didn't find out until he was at the end of his tether, hanging over a precipice and the villain was telling him to cut the rope.

Eastwood visibly did his own climbing and there were the occasional dramatic shots of him in crevasses and on the cliff face. The real stars were the genuine climbers and the photographers.

The hazards of the expedition are spectacularly photographed with the north face of the Eiger looking considerably more dramatic than the north face of Eastwood.

Ian Christie, *Daily Express*

Clint Eastwood's direction is only matched by a performance in the leading role that's about as frozen as the Eiger itself.

Derek Malcolm, *Guardian*

Clint Eastwood and George Kennedy in *The Eiger Sanction*

robbed by a black air stewardess, who turned out to be a spy. The second time, he was nearly murdered by his topless mountain trainer, who had already put him through it. So much for safe sex.

The Eiger Sanction was really two films: one was about mountain-climbing and the other was about spies, and the two never really came

Most depressing, Eastwood directs in a bland, blunt and boorish fashion.

Richard Combs, *Monthly Film Bulletin*

Fortunately, the Eiger resists even Clint Eastwood as star and director. It is bigger than both of him.

Alexander Walker, *Evening Standard*

THE OUTLAW JOSEY WALES

Directed by Clint Eastwood   1976

Josey Wales was a Missouri farmer, living in the
aftermath of the American Civil War, still a time
of blood and dying. His wife and child were
killed, his house burned to the ground and he
himself sabred and left for dead by Union
guerrillas known as Redlegs. At their grave, the
camera framed his grief-stricken face in close-
up to look like a medieval painting of Christ
collapsing under the weight of the cross he was
erecting. Josey, a man of peace, turned avenging
angel and joined a band of Confederate
irregulars on the rampage, hell-bent on putting
things right with summary executions.

The prologue, brilliantly edited by Ferris
Webster, gave way to impressionistic credit
titles: a fleeting, monochromatic, smoky
montage of the war straight out of Matthew
Brady. The colour gradually seeped into the
frame only when the story proper began, an
effect which brought back memories of the
opening of *The Beguiled*.

The prologue was immediately followed by
another memorable sequence when the
renegades, having been promised full amnesty
if they surrendered, were massacred at the very
moment they were pledging their loyalty to the
United States. Josey (who had refused to
surrender) rode in to the rescue, firing his
pistols, and once he had got hold of the Union
machine-gun he killed practically the whole
camp. Of the renegades, only he and a
wounded boy soldier survived.

From then on Josey was hunted by Union
soldiers and bounty hunters alike. There was a
$5,000 reward on his head. 'A man's got to do
something for a living,' said one bounty hunter.
'Dying ain't much of a living,' replied Josey. (If
the film had a message, that was it.) Josey was

Clint Eastwood in *The
Outlaw Josey Wales*

not a hard man to track. He left bodies everywhere, yet somehow he always managed to
escape capture, even when capture looked
most certain. His survival was often hard to
credit. He spat a lot, too, directing black jetties
of tobacco at corpses, dogs, insects and
travelling salesmen. The spittle was his trademark and signature.

Two men in particular were in pursuit of
him, though it could be argued that he was just
as much in pursuit of them as they were of
him. The first was Terrill (Bill McKinney), a
bloodthirsty looter and pillager who had killed
his wife and child and was now a Regular
Federal Authority. The second was his former
friend, Fletcher (John Vernon), who had
betrayed the renegades. Fletcher had been
tricked, but Josey didn't know that.

Clint Eastwood in *The
Outlaw Josey Wales*

There was a good moment of tension when
audiences wondered how he was going to
escape the horse soldiers crossing on the ferry.
The answer was neat and simple: he didn't
attempt to shoot them, he simply shot the
ferry's rope and let them and their horses drift
down the river. William O'Connell was very
funny as the nervous ferryman, hedging his
bets and singing 'Dixie' and 'The Battle Hymn
of the Republic' (the songs of both armies) with
equal enthusiasm.

A sentimental relationship developed
between Josey and the boy soldier (Sam
Bottoms), whose death scene was momentarily
interrupted by two hillbilly bounty hunters
(Len Lesser and Douglas McGrath). Josey didn't
bother to bury them. 'Buzzards got to eat,' he
said, 'same as worms.' Later he would use the
boy's dead body as a decoy, putting it on a
horse and letting it run through the enemy
camp while he made his escape during the
distraction.

A great part of the movie's success was the
casting of Chief Dan George as a wise, old,
white-haired Cherokee called Lone Watie.
Dressed in top hat and frock coat (in order to
look like Abe Lincoln), Watie may have looked
comic but he had enormous dignity. He
belonged, he explained, to one of the so-called
civilized tribes. Indeed, in Washington, the
Second Secretary of the Interior had given the
tribe medals for looking civilized. 'They call us
civilized because we are easy to sneak up on.
The white man has been sneaking up on us for
years. They told us we wouldn't be happy here.
They said we would be happier in the nations.
So they took away our land and sent us here.
We can't trust the white man. I didn't

Clint Eastwood and
Chief Dan George in
The Outlaw Josey Wales

surrender. They took away my horse and made
him surrender.'

When the Cherokees told the Secretary about
their land being stolen and their people dying
(Watie had lost his wife and two sons on 'The
Trail of Tears'), the Secretary exhorted them to
endeavour to survive. The Cherokees thought
about what he had said for a long time and,
when they had thought about it long enough,
they declared war on the Union. The dry
humour and deadpan irony were perfect and
the interplay between Dan George and
Eastwood was a pleasure to watch. The witty,
humane script was based on the novel *Gone to
Texas*, by Forrest Carter who, clear-cut and
simplistic in his attitude to the Comanches,
portrayed them with solemnity and understanding.

There was a dramatic moment at the frontier
town when Josey was recognized by a carpet-
bagger (Woodrow Parfrey) selling phoney

Bill McKinney and
Clint Eastwood in
The Outlaw Josey Wales

medicine for every ailment. 'Well, are you
going to pull those pistols and whistle 'Dixie'?'
he asked five soldiers and, while they dithered,
he shot four of them, leaving the fifth to Lone
Watie.

There were two classic Western images of
Josey. The first had him standing silhouetted in
an open doorway before he dealt with two
traders molesting a squaw. The second had him
standing on a ridge, silhouetted against the sky,
before he rode to the rescue of two Kansas
pilgrims who were being attacked by Coman-
cheros. The granny (Paula Trueman) was a
doughty, bigoted, cartoon-like old lady. Her
daughter (Sondra Locke), who had been
stripped naked and nearly raped, was a simple-
minded, scrawny girl who, predictably, fell in
love with Josey.

They had hardly settled into their new
idyllic home before they were being threatened
by the Comanches. Josey rode out to meet their

chief, Ten Bears (Will Sampson), in order to ward off the attack. 'I say,' he declared in a key line of the script, 'men can live together without butchering each other.' The two men made a blood pact, succeeding where governments had failed.

By treating Josey as a man rather than as a myth, the two women succeeded in turning an avenging angel back into the peace-loving farmer he once had been; but Josey was still an outlaw and he had to move on. As he was leaving the farm, he found Terrill and escort waiting to arrest him. This time it was the pilgrims who came to his rescue. In the final scene he met Fletcher, who affected not to recognize him and told him that he was going to continue his search in Mexico and that when he found Josey Wales, he would tell him that the Civil War was over. 'I guess we all died a little in that damn war,' replied Josey, riding off into the setting sun, a traditional ending, but with one important difference, for he was going back to the farm to begin his life afresh. The story had come full circle.

John Vernon's fine performance as Fletcher had a memorable and much-quoted retort. On being told by the Union commander that 'the spoils of war belonged to the victors', he had replied that there was another well-known saying: 'Don't piss down my neck and tell me it's raining.'

The Outlaw Josey Wales was filmed in a number of breathtaking locations and the changing seasons were stunningly photographed by Bruce Surtees. Jerry Fielding's music was nominated for an Oscar for best original score.

Scratch an Eastwood movie and you'll find a political philosophy three paces to the right of Thomas Jefferson.

Derek Malcolm, *Guardian*

He is not merely part of the landscape. He seems to have grown out of it: a fixture as solid as Monument Valley.

Margaret Hinxman, *Daily Mail*

What is remarkable about the film, however, is the skill with which Eastwood gives this theme a resonantly full orchestration while at the same time silencing any propensities to pretension or sentimentality lurking in the script.

Tom Milne, *Monthly Film Bulletin*

There is nothing in the completion of Wales's full and vicious campaign that justifies all the dramatic headshots and vocal seething – nothing that is except old-fashioned heroics and directorial self-love.

Russell Davies, *Observer*

THE ENFORCER

Directed by James Fargo   1976

Criminals describing themselves as The People's Revolutionary Strike Force were holding San Francisco to ransom. They had enough explosives to blow half the city away and wanted $5 million. They were led by a blue-eyed, ginger-haired, knife-stabbing, gun-blazing psychopath (DeVeren Bookwalter), a dull caricature of a blue-eyed, ginger-haired, knife-stabbing, gun-blazing psychopath.

The Enforcer began with a pre-credit sequence: the murder of two truck drivers. The film proper started with a joke. There was Harry Callahan kicking a man who had just had a heart attack and dragging him out of the restaurant by the scruff of the neck. This seemed a bit rough, even by Harry's normal standards, until it was revealed the man was a professional restaurant pay-dodger who feigned heart attacks. Later, for those who liked that sort of thing, there would be sick jokes during a post-mortem and schoolboy jokes in a massage parlour about customers having a quick lesson in 32 positions of lovemaking with an inflatable doll for $75.

Harry was, as usual, a one-man anti-crime wave, fighting not only criminals but also the police department, bureaucratic blunders, corrupt local government and wet liberals who let crime go unpunished and were willing to pay ransom money when the mayor was kidnapped. Harry, on the other hand, was always ready to meet violence with violence. His ring-wing, chauvinist, sledge-hammer, bulldozing approach to thuggery may not have appealed to everybody, but it undoubtedly continued to strike a cord with audiences, who empathized with one cop's widow. 'It's war, isn't it?' she said at her husband's deathbed.

Clint Eastwood and Albert Popwell in *The Enforcer*

'I guess I never really understood that.'

Callahan had class. He got things done; fuelled by his anger, he never gave up. There was a typical scene when three men were holding hostages in a liquor store. One minute he was spread-eagled on the floor, the next he was driving a car through the shopfront window at them. (As he said, they had asked for a car and he was going to give them one.) The shop, the door, the window, the stock, the shelving, the car and, of course, the hold-up men were a complete write-off. A bill came in to the police department for $14,379. He was reprimanded by his boss for excessive use of force and transferred to personnel division.

Callahan, who treated his new boss, Captain McKay (Bradford Dillman) with exactly the same undisguised contempt he had shown for his previous boss, had a nice line in laconic put-downs: 'Your mouth-wash ain't making it.' McKay, looking after his career and kowtowing to the mayor, pointed out that the minority community had just about had enough with Dirty Harry's dirty methods and he wanted

Tyne Daly and
Clint Eastwood in
The Enforcer

restraint, not a Wild West Show. He was always asking Callahan to hand in his badge and then having to hand it back in an emergency. Harry got on far better with a black militant (Albert Popwell, a stylish actor), who was waiting patiently for the whites to blow each other up.

The mayor (John Crawford), a shallow and devious opportunist, something of a caricature, appointed one of the first full-time women homicide inspectors in America, but only because he thought it would win him votes in the coming election. As a result, Callahan (famed for his misogyny) got lumbered with a woman for a partner. There was an enjoyable moment when he was asked to accept a commendation for something he hadn't done (as part of a photo call for the mayor) and he

told the mayor that the badge was a seven-point suppository and to stick it up his arse.

There was also something endearing about watching Tyne Daly playing cops and robbers, running about, trying to keep up with Harry. She was a good sport and it was not long before she had coaxed some humanity out of him and they were having beers, exchanging *double entendres* and he was paying her pretty compliments. During one of their conversations, she managed to bring up something that most audiences had been meaning to ask for some time but had never dared to ask. 'You're cold, bold Callahan with his great big .44,' she said. 'Every other cop in the city is satisfied with a .38 or .357. What do you have to carry that cannon for? Is it for

penetration?' ('Does everything have to have a sexual connotation for you?' he asked.)

The Enforcer was stronger on comedy than on suspense. There was an over-extended sequence when Callahan was chasing a black suspect down alleys and over rooftops and they both fell through a skylight, landing in a pornographic photographer's studio, which was good for a bit of complimentary nudity. They dashed out into the street and ended up in a church, where the suspect was ultimately caught and knocked out. 'Callahan, I think you are a disgrace to this city!' squalled the priest. The jazz accompaniment, the casting of a comedian as the suspect and the utter lack of urgency made it clear that the chase was not to be taken too seriously, though the man had, in fact, just let off a bomb in a public lavatory.

The climax took place at Alcatraz. The policewoman went the way of all Callahan's partners, taking the bullet while trying to save him. Dying, she found time to apologize: 'Oh, Harry, I messed it up. Don't concern yourself. Kill him!' You could tell how chuffed he was by her death by the way he screamed, 'You fucking fruit!' at the blue-eyed, ginger-haired, knife-stabbing, gun-blazing psychopath and blasted him to smithereens with his enormous bazooka (so much more penetrating than his magnum). Tyne Daly would be reincarnated as Lacey in *Cagney and Lacey*.

As an *homme fatal*, Eastwood is in the Mata Hari class.

Clancy Sigal, *Spectator*

Clint Eastwood in
The Enforcer

Dirty Harry is as exciting to watch as he would be appalling to encounter.

Alan Brien, *Sunday Times*

***The Enforcer* is fairish fun – and certainly no threat to liberal democracy.**

Richard Schickel, *Time*

How can we liberals be so wet? Why don't we go out and shoot something? A decent film, preferably.

Russell Davies, *Observer*

Its sociological conclusions are glib and too easily aligned with fashionable clichés about violence, but director James Fargo winds it all up to a very tight climatic tension.

Tom Hutchinson, *Sunday Telegraph*

THE GAUNTLET

Directed by Clint Eastwood   1977

The Commissioner of Police in Phoenix was hand in glove with the local Mafia and they had provided him with a hooker. What the Commissioner enjoyed most was to get the hooker to strip, lie on her stomach, open her legs, and then, while he pointed a gun at her backside, he masturbated.

The Mafia boss was arrested. So was Gus Mally (the hooker in question), a key witness for the prosecution in the forthcoming trial. The Commissioner, realizing the whole of Arizona would know that he masturbated unless he could stop Mally getting to the witness stand, dispatched a cop to extradite her from prison in Las Vegas and bring her back to Phoenix. He didn't tell the cop how important she was; nor did he inform him that he intended to get them both killed *en route* from the prison to the airport.

The cop was Ben Shockley, an alcoholic, incompetent and discredited. He wasn't very bright, either, and had no idea what was going on; and even after he had gone to a betting shop and found odds of 50–1 were being quoted that the hooker wouldn't make it to the trial, he still couldn't believe he had been set up and that his own people had betrayed him. He changed his mind, though, when the car he had ordered was blown up and cops were chasing them down the highway, shooting to kill. The Commissioner had picked him precisely because he was a drunken bum, a faded number on a rusty badge, and therefore expendable. Fortunately for him, the hooker was brighter than he was. She said she had a degree. (In hooking?).

Clint Eastwood played the dumb cop. Sondra Locke played the foul-mouthed hooker. The dialogue was racy and the sparring was good fun. She called him a big .45 calibre fruit. He punched her in the face. She kicked him in the balls. You knew they were going to fall in love, get married, settle down and have kids. Occasionally, Eastwood and Locke (who were partners in real life) would share a private joke, which audiences could enjoy: 'You don't even know if I am good in bed!' she said. 'I'll take that on faith,' he replied. Eastwood is on record as saying that he never wanted to play Shakespeare, but, on the evidence of their performances here, they would have been well cast in a reworking of *The Taming of the Shrew*, updated to the nineteenth century, set in America and played as a Western.

There was a sequence where they were on a motorbike, which they had stolen from some hippies, and were being pursued by a low-flying helicopter. The action (well photographed by Rexford Metz) was not as thrilling as it should have been, not least because it was unbelievable that the sniper should have kept missing them. You would not have had to have seen many movies to know that the helicopter was going to end up crashing into either the mountain or the pylons and bursting into flames.

Ditching the bike, they jumped on to a moving cattle train, only to find themselves reunited with the hippies, who gave Shockley a terrible beating, using him as they might have used a punchbag. Mally saved him the only way she knew how: by being willing to be raped. (It seemed just the other day that Locke was being raped in the Nevada desert in *The Outlaw Josey Wales*.) Shockley, somehow, managed to recover in time to save her.

Clint Eastwood and
Sondra Locke in
The Gauntlet

The happy pair then hijacked a country bus.
('Good luck!' said a dear little old lady, who
had just been chucked off it.) Once the bus had
been armoured with sheet metal, they ran the
gauntlet of armed police on streets and roofs.
Round upon round of ammunition hit the bus.
Shockley kept driving. When he got a token
wound in the leg, Mally gamely took over. Why
on earth didn't the police shoot the tyres? It
was all so deliberately ludicrous that it was
never exciting. The peppered bus did not
expire until it had climbed the steps of Phoenix
City Hall. It deserved a *Croix de Guerre*
(posthumous). The Commissioner then tried to
kill Shockley, but Mally killed him first.
Shockley lay on the ground, seemingly
mortally wounded. 'I love you! Ben Shockley,
don't you die on me!' she screamed; and, of
course, he didn't.

The Gauntlet was outrageous; yet it had a
serious side, when Mally was explaining that
there was no difference between cops and
whores, except that whores were able to wash
away their filth at the end of the day. The
screenplay also had something to say about the
mindless use of guns. 'Cops are bastards paid
to shoot, not think,' explained the
Commissioner, putting an army of policemen
on the streets; nobody questioned his order.
Again, in a lighter vein, when Shockley
threatened a large group of hippies, Eastwood
had given a parody of how cops are perceived
to behave and talk.

The supporting cast included William Prince
as the blue-eyed, grey-haired, stony-faced
Commissioner, with a voice like the bottom of
a tomb, and Michael Cavanaugh as his corrupt
Assistant District Attorney, who was so bad at

The bus on the steps of
Phoenix Town Hall in
The Gauntlet

His best films, *Josey Wales* and *The Gauntlet* contain sophisticated character interplay within spectacles pitched low to mass audience. He is a cinema, designed more for big box office than for prestige, and in its compromised state is as exciting as it is frustrating.

Tom Allen, *Voice*

The struggle of Clint Eastwood, the director, to escape, subvert or simply have some fun at the expense of Eastwood, the star persona, now amounts to a curious and not unlikeable body of work . . . His personality as a director, however, continues to develop and *The Gauntlet* shows the first signs that he has assimilated the lessons of Don Siegel for the succint, often quasi-humorous delivery of setpieces . . . But what it confirms is that Eastwood hovers on the edge of being one of the most interesting of American directors, if only he could convincingly put down his alter, acting, ego.

Richard Combs, *Monthly Film Bulletin*

As an actor Eastwood is a product of his image rather than the other way round. His success is based on recognizing that fact and ensuring that every performance utilizes it in some way.

Andrew Tudor, *New Society*

Mr Eastwood's talent is his style, unhurried and self-assured.

Vincent Canby, *New York Times*

The only talent involved in this movie belongs to the agent who sold the script (by Michael Butler and Dennis Shryack); the sale price of $500,000 suggests genius.

Pauline Kael, *New Yorker*

his job that his colleagues said 'He couldn't convict Hitler.' Pat Hingle (who had played the Judge in *Hang 'Em High*) was cast as Shockley's old, retired partner, who was used as a decoy and killed by the Attorney's snipers.

One of the key action scenes was the spectacular and comic demolition of the house where Shockley and Mally were hiding out. It was a siege out of *Bonnie and Clyde*. The building was so bullet-ridden that it was absurd they were not killed. When the house finally collapsed, it looked as if it had been eaten away by a gigantic mass of termites. The joke was underlined by the camera cutting to a road sign which read GOD MAKES HOUSE CALLS.

Bill McKinney, one of Eastwood's most regular actors, was cast as a lecherous, sexist cop who taunted Mally. She taunted him back: 'Does your wife know you masturbate?' she enquired. The cop gave a yell of rage, such as Edvard Munch and Francis Bacon would have appreciated. Not long after, mistaken for Shockley, he was ambushed and killed by the Mafia, his car riddled with bullets. So much for masturbators. This time the camera cut to a road sign which read GOD GIVES ETERNAL LIFE.

EVERY WHICH WAY BUT LOOSE

Directed by James Fargo   1978

I've got a feeling Clyde may end up as the star of the film.

Clint Eastwood

Every Which Way But Loose was crude knockout, a silly romp, as broad as it was rowdy. The script was a shambles, the acting was coarse and the direction lumpen.

Clint Eastwood was cast as Philo Beddoe, a good-natured, easy-going, brainless trucker with a working man's taste for cold beer and country music. He gave one woman, who was rash enough to describe the country and western mentality as 'somewhere between moron and dull normal', a set of false teeth in her soup. The humour was at this crude level.

Philo was the best bar-room brawler in town and there was nobody who could hit so fast and so hard. He made money backing himself to beat local fighters. These illegal bare-fisted bouts took place in backyards and workplaces, the dirtiest being in the cold room of a meat factory among the hanging carcasses. The role was a parody of Eastwood's macho prowess.

Philo fell in love with a country and western singer (Sondra Locke) and chased after her from California to Colorado, while he himself was being chased by a motorcycle gang and two Los Angeles cops, whom he had beaten up in one of his many brawls. He was accompanied by his best friend (Geoffrey Lewis) and a girl they had picked up on the highway, plus Clyde, an affectionate, rangy, hairy, floppy-armed, full-grown, 12-stone, male orang-utan from Sumatra that he had won in a fight. Philo looked after his welfare; he not only gave him beers, he also took him to porn shows and to the zoo so that he could get laid. The best

Clint Eastwood and Sondra Locke in *Every Which Way But Loose*

visual joke in the whole movie was Eastwood pretending to shoot him and Clyde pretending to fall down dead. The ape, a seasoned performer from Bobby Borosini's Performing Orang-utan Show, stole most of the notices.

Philo was gauche with women. Confiding in the ape, he said: 'I suppose you think I'm crazy tramping across the country after a girl I hardly even knew. It takes me a long time to get to know a girl; even longer to let her know me. Hell, I'm not afraid of any man, but come to sharing my feelings with a woman, my stomach just turns to royal jelly.' Philo was so dumb, it took him the whole movie to realize that the singer wasn't interested in him at all. She turned out to be a hooker.

All the characters were pretty dumb. Ruth Gordon, rasping away as a tough old lady, was straight out of a strip-cartoon. But nobody was

Clint Eastwood and The Black Widows in *Every Which Way But Loose*

Clint Eastwood and Clyde in *Every Which Way But Loose*

quite as moronic as the middle-aged cycle gang, who had spider tattoos on their arms and their stomachs and called themselves The Black Widows. The gang, who were into leather and Nazi emblems, regularly got beaten up and their bikes were always left in a tangled mess. The actors looked as if they, at least, had had a lot of fun.

For his admirers – of whom I am one – this does nothing to further his reputation at all. In fact it mars it. And, for those who don't know about that reputation, it tells them nothing at all.

Tom Hutchinson, *Sunday Telegraph*

Far from showing off Mr Eastwood to flattering advantage, this kind of format virtually eclipses his talent.

Janet Maslin, *New York Times*

Eastwood thinks that his screen personality is so unshakeable that any amount of self-parody and ridicule cannot tarnish it. He is under a misapprehension.

Nicholas Wapshott, *Scotsman*

Clint comes a cropper.

Philip French, *Observer* headline

ESCAPE FROM ALCATRAZ

Directed by Don Siegel   1979

Alcatraz, a solid rock island a mile from San Francisco, surrounded by treacherous and icy currents, operated as a maximum security prison between 1934 and 1963. In those 29 years, nobody escaped: 39 men tried to get away, 26 were recaptured, seven were shot, three were drowned and three were unaccounted for.

Escape from Alcatraz concerned itself with the three who were unaccounted for, concentrating on Frank Morris (Clint Eastwood). The two brothers, John and Clarence Anglin, were mere ciphers. It was presumed all three had drowned, but their bodies were never found.

Frank Morris arrived at Alcatraz on 18 January 1960, having been transferred from Atlanta. The screenplay told nothing about his background or his crimes. All that was known was that he had escaped from a number of prisons. (Asked what sort of childhood he had had, his answer was 'short'.) He was not scared of anyone, neither inmates, warders nor Warden. His intelligence, patience, nerve and inner strength gave him the edge.

The chilling opening sequence, describing his arrival on the island, was superbly handled by Don Siegel in a series of atmospheric images: the rain lashing down, the impenetrable darkness, the transfer from launch to van, the playing searchlight, the signing in, the medical check, the stripping down, the naked walk down a long corridor of cells. (New arrivals walked naked to their cells; it was designed to humiliate them.) The sequence, photographed by Bruce Surtees and edited by Ferris Webster, is a classic of its kind and got the film off to an excellent start. The cold, impersonal, almost documentary approach

continued, the action punctuated by a recurring image of the bleak island prison glowering in a red sunset.

Escape from Alcatraz was a good box-office title. Siegel, however, was not really that interested in the actual escape; he was much more concerned with the soul-destroying daily routine of the inmates and the effects of imprisonment on them and their warders. The grim conditions were austerely depicted; the convicts' incarceration was a spiritual trial, not a physical one. Every prisoner was confined alone to an individual cell. 'Inmates have no say,' said the megalomaniac Warden. 'They do what they are told. We do not make citizens, but we make good prisoners.' The Warden was not bothered about the men's dignity and rehabilitation; he was unashamedly non-reformative.

The aspects of the escape which did interest Siegel were the physical preparations: the use of nail scissors and stolen spoons; the way false grilles were moulded from stationery and lavatory paper; the way the base of the men's raft was made from raincoats stiffened with contact cement. It was incredible that the escapers' handiwork went undetected. There was only one moment of tension, when it seemed that a warder was going to discover a dummy in the bed and it turned out to be Morris all the time.

Concessions were made to Eastwood's fans: a punch-up in the showers, a near-knifing in the courtyard, some finger-chopping in the carpentry class and a heart attack in the mess. A big brutal homosexual (Bruce M. Fischer, physically gross) propositioned Morris in the showers, which allowed Morris to behave in a

Clint Eastwood in *Escape from Alcatraz*

119

way audiences would expect a Clint Eastwood
movie hero to behave. First, there was a come-
on smile, followed by a gesture implying that
he was going to give the man a hug and then
came the expected lethal blow to the groin and
balls and a bar of soap stuck in his mouth.

Eastwood, leaner and more lined, was at his
most agile in the fights and the final stretches,
creeping around in the darkness, crawling
along the ventilation shaft, clambering over
wire fences, scampering over roofs and sliding
down drainpipes.

There was a performance of great dignity by
Paul Benjamin, who played the proud black
librarian, convicted for the death of two
rednecks he had killed in self-defence. He was
serving two 99-year sentences back to back.
'Sometimes,' he said, 'I think that's all this shit-
hole is, one long count. We count the hours,
the bulls count us and the king bulls count the
counts.'

A major weakness of the movie was the way
the Warden was written and the way he was
acted by Patrick McGoohan. He came across as
a theatrical sadist, given to making smug
remarks: 'Alcatraz was built to keep all the
rotten eggs in one basket. I was specially
chosen to make sure the stink from the basket
doesn't escape.' He was there, primarily, to
read out the prison prospectus and to be
obnoxious to inmates and subordinates alike, a
supercilious figure of authority.

The ending was ambiguous. The Warden
would have preferred to believe the men had
drowned. The cinemagoing public would have
preferred to believe they had escaped. Siegel
pandered to the box office and hinted they
might have got away with a shot of a

chrysanthemum on stony ground. (The flower had been used earlier in the film as a symbol of freedom.) The final image, under the credits, was of a *papier mâché* head, the dummy's grinning face cocking a snook at all those who had believed that nobody could escape from Alcatraz.

A quiet jangling electronic score was used effectively throughout; the only wrong note was the cheap clap of thunder on the line 'Welcome to Alcatraz!' Today the prison is a number one tourist attraction and tourists are just as likely to ask which cell Eastwood occupied as they are to ask about Al Capone.

Clint Eastwood looks every inch a prisoner: in a sense, it is a role he has been playing all his life. His bleakness shines like armour; his face resembles striated granite; his mouth is so thin that only stray monosyllables can squeeze through; he has the wary expression of a man to whom the world is a trap which might suddenly be sprung. He is the professional outsider.

Peter Ackroyd, *Spectator*

He is such a still actor that no one else can get more effect out of a brief, reluctant smile, a sidelong glance or a one-word speech.

David Robinson, *The Times*

Clint Eastwood's flinty and obdurate charisma makes one feel he would be better cast as the prison itself rather than as the convict trying to escape therefrom . . . Eastwood walks through it all tall, cool and monolithic, looking more and more with each film as if it can only be a matter of time before he joins the geological immortals on Mount Rushmore.

Nigel Andrews, *Financial Times*

At the time when Hollywood entertainments are more overblown than ever, Eastwood proves that less really can be more.

Frank Rich, *Time*

Mr Eastwood fulfils the demands of the role and of the film as probably no other actor could. Is it acting? I don't know, but he's a towering figure in its landscape.

Vincent Canby, *New York Times*

Clint Eastwood and Larry Hankin in *Escape from Alcatraz*

The 1980s

Clint Eastwood in
Pale Rider

BRONCO BILLY

Directed by Clint Eastwood   1980

Bronco Billy, good-natured and likeable, funny and touching, was an American fable about the American dream. 'You can be anything you want,' said a member of the Bronco Billy Wild West Show. 'All you have to do is to go out and become it.'

'Everybody loves cowboys and clowns, you're everybody's hero for a while,' sang Ronnie Milsap during the opening credits; and nobody wanted to be a cowboy more than Billy McCoy, a former shoe salesman who had been raised in a one-room tenement building in New Jersey and had never seen a horse till he was 31 years old. The only cowboy he had seen had been in the movies.

Billy lived a life of fantasy as a sharp-shooting, knife-throwing, stunt-riding cowboy in a tacky travelling show. Billed as the greatest hip-shooter, the fastest draw in the West, the only time he behaved like a real, live cowboy was when he managed to foil a bank robbery; and nobody was more surprised than he was. The screenplay was an affectionate lampoon at the expense of the clichés of the Wild West, while Billy himself was a caricature of Eastwood's macho persona.

Billy had picked up his troupe while he was in prison, serving a sentence for attempting to murder his wife, whom he had discovered in bed with his best friend. The troupe, a team of losers and no-hopers, all down on their luck, included: a doctor (Scatman Crothers) who had practised without a licence and was now the MC; a former bank teller (Bill McKinney) who had robbed the bank and was a one-armed, hook-handed roustabout; a Vietnam war deserter (Sam Bottoms) who twirled a rope; a Red Indian (Dan Vadis) who kept getting bitten

Bill McKinney and
Clint Eastwood in
Bronco Billy

by his rattlesnake; and his squaw (Sierra Pecheur). They played to sparse audiences.

Billy, gentle, genial, kind-hearted, loyal to his team, was the best friend man ever had. He was charity itself, putting on free shows in orphanages, hospitals and mental institutions, and was loved by children, nuns, doctors and inmates alike. He had an old-fashioned, family-values morality ('You should never kill a man unless it's absolutely necessary') and he was liable, at the drop of a stetson, to mouth homely platitudes and preach against hard liquor and cigarettes. He was a kid at heart, a big kid in a man's body. His troupe loved him and they hadn't been paid in six months. When he addressed them, he sounded like he was addressing the nation.

Far and away the most dramatic exchange, partly because it was so unexpected and so uncharacteristic of an Eastwood hero, was when the local sheriff (Walter Barnes, excellent casting), a nasty bit of work, taunted Billy, forcing him to admit that he was no good and Billy, instead of beating him to pulp, allowed himself to be humiliated (and paid a bribe he could ill-afford) in order to get the Vietnam deserter out of prison.

Sondra Locke was cast as an arrogant, spoiled, headstrong New York heiress, described by her husband as a 'cold-blooded viper' and ditched by him on their honeymoon. It was a marriage of convenience; she needed to marry somebody, *anybody*, before she was 30 in order to inherit her father's fortune. The heiress was a typical Capraesque heroine, running away from herself.

There was a funny performance by Geoffrey Lewis as the frustrated groom, a wimpish termite who had married the heiress for her money and was sorely tried on his wedding night. 'Sometimes she makes me so mad I could kill her!' Denied his conjugal rights, he ran off the next morning with her car, money, clothes and jewellery.

Stranded without a cent to her name, the heiress found herself, most unwillingly, spread-eagled on a death-defying, revolving wheel of fortune and popped at with bullets and knives by a blindfolded Billy. Their romantic battle was stormy. (Locke brought a sharp, sarcastic edge to the banter.) Finally, of course, everything came up roses and she and Billy were rolling about together. 'Take it easy,' he said – and here Eastwood and Locke shared a private joke – 'we've got the rest of our lives to enjoy each other.'

There was a punch-up in a bar which seemed to be just there for the sake of a punch-up and was clearly aimed at the redneck audience who had enjoyed the brawls in *Every Which Way But Loose*. There was also a near-rape in a car park for no other reason, it would seem, than Sondra Locke always got nearly raped in a Clint Eastwood movie.

A much more original scene, and more relevant to the movie's theme, was a botched train robbery. Billy had decided to rob the train after their big tent had burnt down and they hadn't the money to buy a new one. As they rode alongside, absurdly firing their guns and shooting their arrows, the train whizzed past, totally ignoring them. 'You're living in a dream world,' observed the heiress. 'There are no more cowboys and Indians. That's in the past.'

When the heiress disappeared, and was presumed murdered by the groom, a crooked

lawyer persuaded the groom to plead temporary insanity, confess to the murder and go to a mental institution. A bribe of half a million dollars was very persuasive, and since he looked like an idiot anyway, he had no difficulty in convincing the nutty-looking principal of the asylum that he was insane. The principal had a nice line when welcoming visitors: 'You can take your meals with the staff, or the patients, whichever you feel more comfortable with.' The inmates sewed Billy a big tent made entirely from Stars and Stripes flags. This ironically patriotic finish to the movie was followed by Billy's folksy message to all the 'little pardners': 'I want you to finish your oatmeal at breakfast. Do as your ma and pa tell you, because they know best. Don't ever tell a lie and say your prayers at night before you go to bed.'

Clint Eastwood is one of the most vital forces in contemporary American cinema and only the foolish continue to ignore, patronize or dismiss him. As actor, producer and director, he rarely fails to astonish.

Philip French, *Observer*

Only the autocracy and independence conferred by such supreme stardom and command of the box office could permit him to make such an odd, unfashionable, self-deprecating and wholly attractive film as *Bronco Billy*.

David Robinson, *The Times*

There are few enough stars around who can so mock their own image, as he does here, and yet keep it intact by the fervency of an approach that shows that beneath those satirized values are others that are just as worthwhile.

Tom Hutchinson, *Now*

Clint Eastwood in
Bronco Billy

ANY WHICH WAY YOU CAN

Directed by Buddy Van Horn   1980

Clint Eastwood in *Any Which Way You Can*

Any Which Way You Can was the mixture as before, only rougher: a coarse, mindless entertainment, aimed at the redneck box office and appealing to the lowest common denominator. It was worse than *Every Which Way But Loose*.

Cast once more as Philo Beddoe, the toughest bare-knuckle fighter in the country, Clint Eastwood stripped to the waist and knuckled down to it. He was in good shape and no jaw was left unsocked. The movie was one long punch-up, ending with an epic brawl in the John Ford manner: a bruising, illegal, bare-knuckle fight, fought out by two rivals who had become friends and watched by a hysterical and drooling crowd of men and women. Described as the fight of the century, it went on for ever. Philo won, despite a broken arm.

Sondra Locke and Clint Eastwood in *Any Which Way You Can*

'I can take pain,' he said, 'but not love pains.' Sondra Locke was again on hand in her role of country and western singer, but her character had been softened out of all recognition. She was no longer a hooker ('I didn't mean to hurt you. I was mixed-up') and was totally unfazed when she discovered Philo in bed with an ape. 'I think I love you,' she said. 'I think that's a piece of luck for me,' said Philo.

Clyde, the orang-utan, looked different. He was different; the original ape was no longer available. The wags said he had seen the script and turned it down. (Actually, he had died.) The new Clyde dismantled Cadillacs (even while people were still in them) and had a nasty habit of defecating in police cars.

The supporting cast remained unchanged. Geoffrey Lewis was Philo's best friend and Ruth Gordon, still over-acting, was irascible, rasping, dotty Ma. The moronic, bungling, middle-aged bikers were now bald and wearing wigs. The slapstick was as crude as ever, but just to show how nice they really were, underneath all the neo-Nazism, they saved Beddoe from getting shot by the Mob, a scene which was no more convincing than the one where Clyde saved Philo from a burning car. The only remotely funny incident was when, having been drenched in oil, the gang stiffened up and keeled over one by one.

Any Which Way You Can was chiefly notable for its vulgarity, especially in the motel, with four couples making love at the same time. There was Eastwood and Locke in one room. There was an elderly couple, who hadn't had sex in years, in another room. There were two apes in a third room. (Both Clyde and Philo were discovered hanging from the light

Clyde and Clint
Eastwood in *Any Which
Way You Can*

fittings.) And if this were not enough, there was octogenarian Ruth Gordon seducing a Peeping Tom.

The most enjoyable moment came right at the beginning, listening to Eastwood singing a song he had written over the credit titles.

Eastwood, who can be a compelling, charming screen actor, seems content here to watch the other performers pamper their eccentricities while he stands off to one side, as glum and immobile as a Teamster's ashtray.

Richard Curliss, *Time*

As tribute to the virtues of beer-swilling, fist-clenching, isolationist Middle America, they may cheer Reagan voters, but, by God, they frighten me.

Alan Brien, *Sunday Times*

It's a knockabout comedy directed by Buddy Van Horn, who would appear to have the sense of humour of a hippopotamous and the sensitivity of a jackboot.

Ian Christie, *Daily Express*

They say actors should never work with animals or children. In this case, it's apes who shouldn't work with Clint Eastwood. He dominates the film with his personality and the easy comic touch of a true star.

Alan Frank, *Daily Star*

I hope I never meet anyone who actually likes such a trashy experience.

Alexander Walker, *Evening Standard*

HONKYTONK MAN

Directed by Clint Eastwood   1982

Honkytonk Man, part romantic weepie, part rite of passage, was a picaresque odyssey from Oklahoma to Tennessee. The story was set in the 1930s and came out of Clint Eastwood's own experience of the Depression years, the opening dust-storm sequence recalling John Ford's film of John Steinbeck's *The Grapes of Wrath*.

Eastwood has described the hero, Red Stovall, an untalented country and western singer, as somebody who never believed in himself and seemed actively to seek out his failure. Red made his entrance in a battered limousine; he was dead drunk, broke and all he had was a guitar, a bottle of whiskey and the clothes he was wearing. He was terminally ill with tuberculosis and should have been in a sanatorium. He covered his fear with improvised bravado and good-humoured self-mockery, always the first to admit he was a no-good bastard.

Intent on living his life on his own terms, Red was still in pursuit of his dream to be somebody before he died and was heading south for the Grand Ole Opry audition in Nashville. His sister (a fine performance by Verna Bloom, who looked as if she had stepped out of a photograph of the period) asked her 14-year-old son, Whit, to accompany him, not wanting him to go alone. Whit, a freckled farmboy who idolized his uncle and became his minder, was played by Eastwood's own son, Kyle.

The action was set mainly on the road and there were stopovers in honkytonks, flophouses, cheap hotels, jails, dives and, finally, a recording studio. The journey was a series of comic encounters, punctuated by songs, such

Kyle Eastwood and Clint Eastwood in *Honkytonk Man*

as the very appealing 'Honkytonk Man' ('Throw your arms round the honkytonk man/We'll get through the night the best way we can') and 'One fiddle, two fiddle, three fiddle'.

Many of the interludes were included for Eastwood's regular fans. The first was when uncle and nephew stole chickens and got caught. Red was body-searched in the street by two unpleasant cops and then arrested after he had asked them if it gave them a thrill to grope a man's crotch. Whit (inspired by a poster for a Western called *When a Man Sees Red*) effected his rescue by attaching a rope to the car and the bars of a cell window and driving off, pulling the wall down. Shortly afterwards, a raging bull attacked Red. The bull did not take kindly to Red having a bath in his drinking water.

There was a delightful incident when Whit was driving the car and they were stopped by a

highway patrolman (Tim Thomerson). Whit, being underage, naturally didn't have a licence. The patrolman, pocketing a bribe, insisted man and boy should change places; but as he watched Red driving down the road, veering from left to right, he drove after them and suggested it would be better if the boy drove the car after all.

There was also a very amusing scene when a robbery went wrong. The idea was that Red would pretend to stick up an old lady who ran a diner. He would get the cash in the till and she would claim the money from the insurance. The only trouble was that the old lady hadn't been warned Red was coming and got completely hysterical, screaming her head off.

When they finally reached Nashville, Red collapsed in the middle of his audition. The promoters turned him down, not wanting him coughing up his lungs on a national radio show. The doctor said he shouldn't even be singing in a shower. When he was offered a record deal ($20 a song), he took it, knowing it was his last chance. He collapsed again during the recording session, while singing 'Honky-tonk Man', and was unable to finish. Eastwood, coughing blood, his face completely ravaged, was very convincing.

Honkytonk Man was an opportunity for Eastwood to work with his son and, of course, their special relationship, understated and touching, was to the advantage of Clancy Carlile's screenplay; but Kyle's limited acting ability was obvious. The face was blank too often and his scenes lacked spontaneity.

John McIntire, cast as the genial grandpa, gave a vivid account of a bit of American history, remembering how, as an 18-year-old,

Clint Eastwood and
Alexa Kenin in
Honkytonk Man

he and hundreds of other white settlers had
taken part, on 16 September 1893, in the
greatest horserace for the greatest prize, The
Cherokee Strip. 'It wasn't just the land, just the
dirt itself, I was racing for. It wasn't just the
land, it was the dream. It wasn't just land-
chasers, it was dream-chasers. Look at it. All
turned to dust. We ruined it.'

Alexa Kenin played a crazy girl who wanted
to be a singer. There was a tiny problem. She
couldn't sing. There was a whole gallery of
cameo roles, all nicely acted: Barry Corbin as a
lying, cheating promoter, a fat porky son of a
bitch who owed Red $100; Susan Peretz as a
brothel madam; Steve Autry as a moronic
mechanic; Jerry Hardin and Gary Grubbs as the
arresting cops; and Joe Regalbuto as the talent
scout who gave Red his final job.

This is a lovingly tempered, discreetly eloquent
piece of moviemaking that is very close to the
masterpiece that Eastwood must one day make . . .
Honkytonk Man is arcane, classic Americana, and,
so help me, it's not far short of magnificent.

Richard Cook, *New Musical Express*

It is a solid, well-crafted piece of folksy Americana
that might have succeeded even better had it stayed
even truer to its melancholic instincts.

Philip Bergson, *What's On*

Eastwood tries to sustain the music with his voice
which is charming and whispery, but just too thin to
flesh out this film.

Carrie Rickey, *Voice*

The film comes across sympathetically but
unconvincingly as an attempt by a well-established
movie guy to reveal his tender side.

Janet Maslin, *New York Times*

The sentiment is so laid-back that it ensconces you
in an uncritical coma, perhaps because the movie
feels very much at home with its aims – or with the
narcissistic self-mockery that is the spirit of Clint
Eastwood's direction of himself. Yet it's a straight-
up, four-square, honest, old-style production that
disarms us all.

David Hughes, *Sunday Times*

FIREFOX

Directed by Clint Eastwood   1982

'I don't believe it!' said one of the characters. He was not alone. *Firefox*, a mixture of science fiction and propaganda, based on Craig Thomas's best-selling novel, was immensely long and immensely dull. Clumsily scripted, lacking continuity and coherence, it told an implausible and politically naïve story without suspense and thrills. There was so much exposition at the beginning that the editors clearly got worried; their fidgety editing, however, only made things worse.

Clint Eastwood was cast at Mitchell Gant, a Vietnam veteran, a retired ace flyer, reluctantly pressed back into service to carry out a suicide mission. His superiors tried a bit of flattery ('They still talk about you . . . we need you, major, you're the best we got') and a bit of blackmail, threatening to take away his land if he didn't agree. However, given his mental history it was very odd that American Intelligence should even have considered him for the job. Gant was still shell-shocked, haunted by memories of burning children in Vietnam and liable to become a twitching neurotic at the most inconvenient of moments.

Firefox was the codename for the greatest war plane ever built. The Russians had invented a deadly supersonic fighter which couldn't be detected by radar. It was operated by thought waves and could fly at six times the speed of sound. Gant's job was to steal it. Could he bring it off? He could speak Russian. But the big question was, could he *think* in Russian? He was smuggled into the USSR and once there he kept changing his identity, donning numerous disguises (businessman, tourist, driver's mate) for no good dramatic reason. There was only one genuine moment of

Clint Eastwood in *Firefox*

anxiety and that was when he was trying to avoid the KGB on Moscow's underground and murdered one of their number in a public lavatory.

His task, which had begun by being ridiculously difficult, suddenly became ridiculously easy the moment he got to the aerodrome and he was able to fly the fighter out of the hangar before anybody could say 'Biggles!' His transformation to *Boy's Own* hero was instant. The US Defense Secretary Caspar Weinberger was quoted as saying that he thought *Firefox* was exciting and good for morale because the Americans won.

The grand finale (accompanied by Maurice Jarre's patriotic music) took place over the Arctic. Gant was pursued by a Russian pilot whose plane he had pinched. The dogfight was not thrilling, mainly because, with a visor over his head, it could have been anybody in the cockpit and it didn't seem to make a scrap of difference whether Gant could think in Russian or not. The special effects by John Dykstra were disappointing, too. There were some pretty

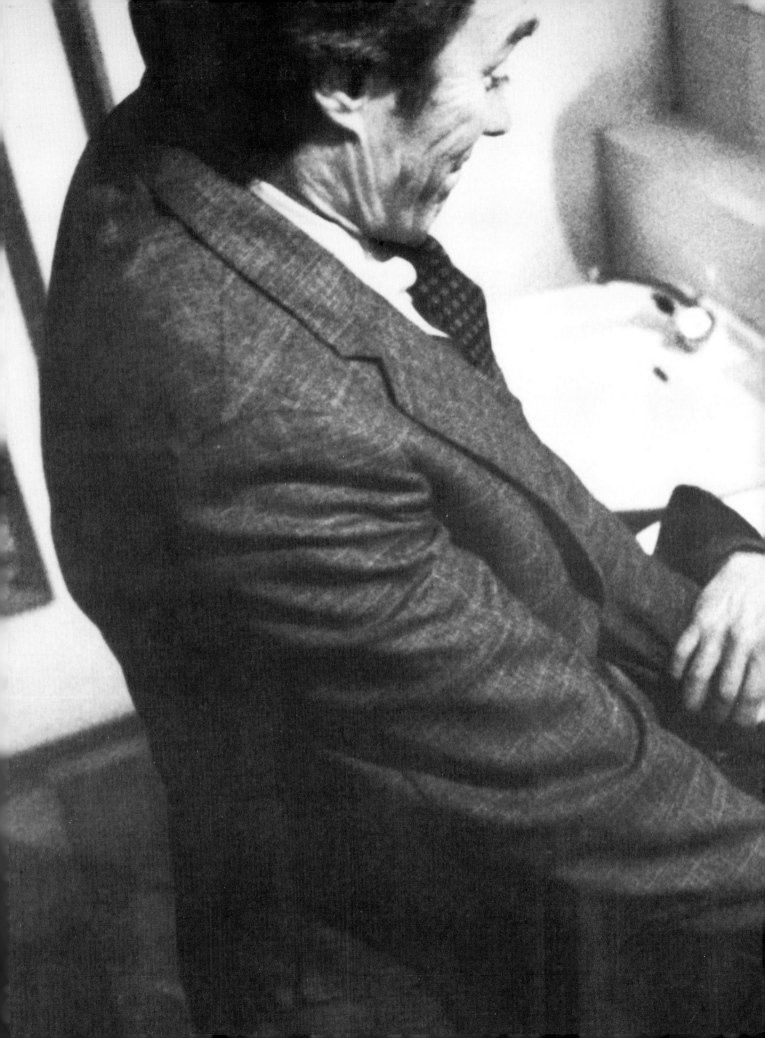

Clint Eastwood and
Eugene Lipinski in
Firefox

pictures of snow and water shooting up, but
much of the action, especially when he was
flying through ravines, was a straight crib from
Dykstra's work in *Star Wars*.

There was so much bad writing, so much bad
acting and so many bad accents that the
Russians emerged as cartoon caricatures,
incompetent stereotypes, squabbling like a lot
of children. The use of Russian first names
only added to the general phoniness. Stefan
Schnabel, cast as the First Secretary of the
Communist Party, was made up to look like
Brezhnev. One minute he was making sensible
criticisms of American foreign policy ('They
are simply paying the price for years of
softness') and being philosophical ('If the roles
were reversed we would have acted similarly').
The next minute he was blowing his top.

Kenneth Colley, hollow-cheeked and sunken-
eyed, cast as a nasty Russian officer, behaved
in the way nasty German officers used to
behave in World War II movies. As for Freddie
Jones, let loose as an eccentric British
Intelligence officer, he rolled his eyeballs in a
manner which even Robert Newton might have
found excessive. Everybody, Russians,
Americans and Brits, spoke in clichés. The
dialogue was, unintentionally, very funny.
There were crass references to Vietnam and
Jewish dissidents who went willingly to their
deaths for Gant. 'Why are you prepared to die?'
he asked. 'It's a small thing compared to my
resentment of the KGB,' replied one scientist
(Nigel Hawthorne) before being mown down by
a hail of bullets.

Eastwood, ice-cold, displayed none of his
usual charisma. He looked worried and
careworn throughout, as if his mind were

Clint Eastwood in *Firefox*

elsewhere, more preoccupied with the production than the direction, the acting and his own performance. The best part was the opening sequence, before the story proper began, when Gant was being tracked by a helicopter as he jogged in his country retreat.

For simple-mindedness of attitudes, bungling confusion of narrative, and solid-from-the-neck-up actors, Clint Eastwood's *Firefox*, featuring himself as producer, director and star, can have few rivals.

Alan Brien, *Sunday Times*

As a study of a man hollowed out to a shell of instinctive responses, Eastwood sometimes looks too good for his own film.

Richard Cook, *New Musical Express*

It's a James Bond movie without girls, a Superman movie without a sense of humour.

Vincent Canby, *New York Times*

Gant, I fear, is a symbolic figure. He is meant to be America itself, traumatized by Nam, and the movie appears to be Clint's shot in the arm for a country that (as the jargon goes) 'has lost its will' to fight Communism.

David Denby, *New York Magazine*

As a cynical piece of political subversion, it's a classic. The sort of thing we've always been warned about.

Mike Parker, *The Leveller*

SUDDEN IMPACT

Directed by Clint Eastwood   1983

People are a bit edgy about the rights of the criminal taking precedence over the rights of the victims. They are more impatient with courtroom procedures and legal delays. I think the public is interested in justice and that's what Harry stands for. He is unique because he stood for the same principles from the beginning, when it wasn't terribly fashionable.

Clint Eastwood

It was in *Sudden Impact* that Harry Callahan, famously, invited a robber to draw his gun on him. 'Go ahead,' he said, 'make my day.' The line immediately passed into common currency.

Seven years on, Callahan was still up against hoodlums, lily-livered liberals and his superiors. The film began with a female judge dismissing a case and the villains being set free because the evidence was inadmissible. The lads left the courtroom, laughing. San Francisco was crumbling under shootings, knifings and beatings. Old ladies were being bashed over their heads for their social security cheques. Teachers were being thrown out of fourth-floor windows because they didn't give As.

Callahan waded through the scum of a city being swept away by bigger and bigger waves of corruption, apathy and red tape. Seven years on, not surprisingly, he looked older, greyer, worn, tired. The face was tight as a mask. The brow was creased. There were new, deeper lines. The blood vessels throbbed. He still did what he had to do, though his successes were often more costly to the city and the department in terms of bad publicity and physical destruction than other people's failures. 'Harry is a real class act,' said his

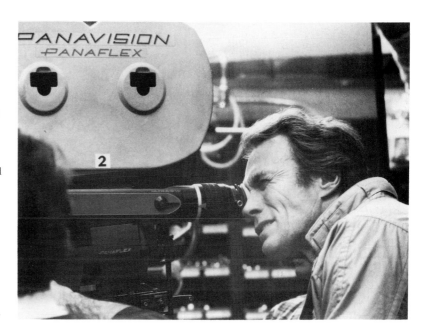

Clint Eastwood previews a shot in *Sudden Impact*

admirers. 'You're a dinosaur,' said his denigrators. 'Your ideas don't fit any more.'

Invading a wedding party, Callahan harassed the bride's grandfather, one of the city's biggest crime lords (the man sounded like a relation of Marlon Brando's Godfather) and caused him to have a heart attack. His bosses decided to dispatch him to San Paulo, a seaside resort, to help solve a local murder case. He had barely arrived when he spotted a bank robber and gave chase. The man jumped on a bike. Callahan jumped into the driver's seat of a senior citizens' bus. The pensioners egged him on: 'Chase his arse! Nail the son of a bitch!' they cried. 'The best day trip I had since they dumped me into that home,' said one old man.

Asked by Callahan why he was dragging his feet on the case, the San Paulo chief of police (Pat Hingle) replied he was dealing with mugging, shoplifting, burglaries, drunken

Clint Eastwood in
Sudden Impact

driving (the crimes which didn't grab the headlines), and that he was doing the best he could. 'Perhaps, it's not good enough,' said Harry, whose search for the murderer was complicated by the Mob's attempts on his life.

There was nobody Callahan could trust, except for his black partner (who, naturally, went the way of all his partners) and a young local cop (Mark Keyloun) who, contrary to all expectations, was still alive at the end of the movie. The casting of Albert Popwell as the partner may have succeeded in tricking some cinemagoers, who had seen him play the minder in *Coogan's Bluff*, the robber in *Dirty Harry*, the pimp in *Magnum Force* and the militant in *The Enforcer*, into thinking, on his first entrance, as he crept up on a target-practising Harry, that he was a hired killer.

Sudden Impact had opened with a love scene in a car in a deserted spot. The woman (Sondra Locke) undid the man's flies and then

shot him in the balls. (This is what you would call a .38 vasectomy and it is not to be recommended.) She then shot him in the head. Ten years previously she and her younger sister had been raped. Her sister had ended up in an institution. She had come back to kill all those who had been responsible. The murders were punctuated by lingering, graphic flashbacks of the two women's ordeal. Her vendetta recalled François Truffaut's *La Mariée était en noir* (*The Bride Wore Black*). There was a particularly good scene when she refused to listen to one pleading victim (well played by Wendell Wellman) who was now a respectable local businessman. Sondra Locke, sharp of feature, wan of complexion, her hair cascading down, looked as if she were understudying Veronica Lake in a 1940s *film noir*.

Callahan, as always, believed in the law of the gun and that crime should be punished. The murderess was of the same opinion. 'This is the age of lax responsibilities and defeated justice,' she argued. 'What happens now? What exactly are my rights? And where was all the concern when I was being beaten and mauled? What about my sister's rights when she was brutalized? There is a thing called justice and was it justice that they all should walk away?' Cop and murderess (though at the time he did not know she was the murderess) shared the same beliefs and the same bed and, at the end of the film, he did not arrest her.

Clint Eastwood's production had a dark, sinister quality; much of the movie was shot at night. The final nine minutes were staged in a empty fairground. (Fairgrounds are always good value.) Callahan was discovered on the broadwalk, looking for all the world like a lawman in a Western, ready for the final shoot-out. 'Holy shit!' said one of the gang, as well he might, for there, unmistakably, was The Man With No Name reincarnated, an avenging angel in silhouette, his gun by his side and so dramatically lit that the lights had given him a halo. The darkness, the close-ups, the music and the editing were all first-rate.

Paul Drake played the raucous, cackling, crazy, impotent gang leader, attempting to out-Cagney Cagney, before he fell to his death, impaled (phallic justice, this) on an outsize horn of a carousel unicorn. Audrie J. Neenan was memorably cast as a foul-mouthed lesbian. There was also, regrettably, a farting bulldog, strayed in from another picture by mistake.

What Harry Callahan represents is not only ruthlessness but a sinister form of impatience and you don't have to be a fascist to be guilty of that.

Michael Wood, *New Society*

Albert Popwell and Clint Eastwood in *Sudden Impact*

No amount of skilful crafting can disguise the fact that this is a glib, meretricious movie, and, particularly from a film-maker of Eastwood's proven ability, a reprehensible one.

David Castell, *Sunday Telegraph*

And it is the contemptuous assumption that this blood-soaked bully is to be regarded as a fit hero for our times and box office that makes this such an ugly movie.

Tom Hutchinson, *Mail on Sunday*

By any standard Eastwood is a Hollywood great and in this film he is on firm ground. Doing what his fans want him to do – killing people. Liberals will cringe – Harry Callahan is anathema to them – but morally reprehensible or not, *Sudden Impact* is terrific entertainment.

William Russell, *Glasgow Herald*

One of the most unpleasant, reactionary and cruel pictures it has been my misfortune to see.

Ian Bell, *Scotsman*

I like Eastwood, always have. But then I have a soft spot in my heart for law and order.

Andrew Sarris, *Voice*

TIGHTROPE

Directed by Richard Tuggle   1984

There is a darkness inside all of us. You, me and the man down the street. Some have it under control. Others act it out. The rest of us try to walk a tightrope between the two.

A psychiatrist in the film

Tightrope, a disturbing psychological drama, was sometimes described as the thinking man's *Dirty Harry*. The real subject matter this time was not law and order but sex and violence; and the subject was a risky one for a major star, because it soon became apparent that the violence was part of the turn-on.

Clint Eastwood was cast as Wes Block, a big city cop investigating a series of sadistic killings. There were, he pointed out, a possible 120,000 suspects. What made the movie so absorbing was that in searching for the murderer the cop found himself. The killer forced him to confront his own impulses. Sexually hungry, Wes sought relief with prostitutes and had developed a taste for bondage. (Since he was a cop he used handcuffs.) One by one, the prostitutes he visited were murdered. The man he was stalking was stalking him, acting out his desires, even tricking him into dating a male prostitute:

Man: He said you would like it.
Wes: Well, he's wrong.
Man: Why don't you try it?
Wes: Maybe I have.

The killer and the cop could so easily have been the same person; it was the uncertainty which gave the film its tension. *Tightrope*, in this respect, was not unlike *This Story of Yours*, a play by John Hopkins, which had been seen briefly at the Royal Court Theatre,

London, and which was later filmed by Sidney Lumet and starred Sean Connery.

Wes was a single parent, with two young daughters. His wife had left him because he had treated her too tenderly; she, it seemed, had also wanted the rough stuff. 'What's a hard-on, daddy?' asked his youngest child. The older (played by Eastwood's own daughter, Alison) sniggered at her father's discomfort.

Richard Tuggle's screenplay explored Wes's relationship not only with the prostitutes and his children but also with a counsellor (the admirable Geneviève Bujold) who ran the New Orleans Rape Crisis Centre. He made a pass over the oysters. ('I was wondering what it would be like to lick the sweat off your body.') They shared a work-out at the gymnasium which *sounded* like they were having sex. Later he had a wet dream about her, which was cleverly photographed from her point of view so that cinemagoers were fooled into thinking she really was being attacked by the killer.

Eastwood, haunted and hunted, deadbeat and ravaged, looked his age: a vulnerable, lonely man, struggling to cope with the darker side of his personality. His encounters drew him deeper and deeper into a sordid world and Tuggle, not averse to using the occasional blatant sexual imagery (such as bottles ejaculating all over the place in a bottle factory), made excellent use of New Orleans's Red Light district, with its dives, bars, brothels, massage parlours and topless dancers, go-go boys, women wrestlers and hookers. Lennie Niehaus provided a nice jazz score accompaniment.

There was a typical Hitchcockian scene when Wes was in a deserted warehouse full of huge carnival heads, looking for the murderer,

Clint Eastwood and Geneviève Bujold in *Tightrope*

and found the male prostitute hanging from the rafters. There was a foreseeable assault on his home. His 12-year-old daughter was tied up and nearly raped, the family pets were killed and, for an extra bit of horror, the housekeeper was murdered and stuffed into the washing machine.

There was enough lightning in the final night-chase sequence for a Gothic melodrama. A police helicopter's harsh spotlight picked out the killer as he fled through a graveyard, past the mausoleums and into the railyard, pursued by Wes. The two men fought it out on the tracks. The scene ended with the killer's arm being severed by an on-coming train, an unnecessary bit of *grand guignol.*

If only Mr Eastwood could be persuaded to stay away from lucrative junk and stick to films of this quality the cinematic world would be a better place.

Ian Bell, *Scotsman*

Tightrope offers more intricacy, suspense and atmospheric color than most of Eastwood's gumshoe safaris through the urban jungle. More important, it represents a provocative advance in the consciousness, self and social, of Eastwood's one-man genre.

Richard Schickel, *Time*

More and more he's beginning to look like the last serious man in Hollywood.

David Denby, *New York Magazine*

He's never completely convincing in his quest for the heart of sexual darkness. It's the penalty he pays for the moral strength he projects on the surface. Whatever lies underneath it is very unlikely to be sneaky or perverted.

Andrew Sarris, *Voice*

He seems to want to be fiery, but he doesn't have it in him – there's no charge in his self-disgust.

Pauline Kael, *New Yorker*

CITY HEAT

Directed by Richard Benjamin   1984

City Heat was a send-up of a typical Warner Brothers gangster movie, set in 1932, during the Prohibition era, the date pinpointed by a scene taking place in the crowded foyer of a cinema showing the Marx Brothers' *Horse Feathers*.

The period was lovingly re-created by designer Edward Carfango. The characters met in speakeasies, boxing rings, bordellos and studio-bound rainy streets. (It never stopped raining.) The thugs wore flat caps, the prostitutes wore cloche hats and the table lamps wore art-deco shades. There were those who thought the director, Richard Benjamin, had paid more attention to period detail than he had to the drama.

The film was originally called *Kansas City Jazz* and was intended to be directed by Blake Edwards and have songs. It should have been a good-humoured lark, tongue-in-cheek and zany; and it was, but the script, broad, mechanical and facetious, was never good enough. The repartee was weak, rarely rising above banality ('Next time, I'm going to knock you so hard, back into the Stone Age, where you came from') and mere vulgarity ('You're supposed to slush that, not smoke it'). The pace constantly sagged. The were too many unpleasant killings. Songs would have been a good idea.

Clint Eastwood and Burt Reynolds played rival detectives, two former buddies, now bosom enemies, constantly at loggerheads, their amiable, aggressive banter tempered by mutual respect. Lieutenant Speer (Eastwood) had remained in the force. Mike Murphy (Reynolds) had resigned and was running a non-profitable detective agency. Speer, grim-faced, hard-boiled, tight-lipped, ignored any mayhem that

might be going on around him, until it affected him personally, when he would develop a manic facial tic and go berserk. Reynolds looked like a typical 1930s gigolo. Everything about him was in period: his face, his moustache, his toupee, his teeth, his buttonhole, his cigarette dangling from his mouth, his soft chamois-coloured hat, his tailored suits, his macintosh. Murphy was the dapperest of dapper ladies' men, a narcissistic, wise-cracking, cowardly rogue, oozing charm. Reynolds played him with self-mocking vanity and cocky cuteness. *City Heat* was his movie.

The film opened with a comic fight in a luncheonette with Speer sitting by while his former buddy was being beaten to a pulp and doing nothing about it, until his coffee was spilt. Later, there was some quasi-serious fighting on the landing of a tenement building.

Burt Reynolds and Clint Eastwood in *City Heat*

'Everything all right?' asked a tenant, coming out of his room after minutes of gunfire. 'All right for me, not so good for him,' replied Speer, who had just shot a man dead.

The major set-piece was an extended street battle with everybody blasting away with a never-ending supply of ammunition. Vintage cars had their windscreens, headlights and petrol tanks riddled with bullets. Speer sat in his car and did nothing until a bullet hit his windscreen and then, suddenly, there he was – beautifully framed within the arc of shooting water from a burst street pump – walking down the centre of the street, indestructible, firing his gun, as if he were Clint (The Man With No Name) Eastwood back in the Old West of Sergio Leone. The sequence ended with Speer punching Murphy on the jaw when Murphy, who had been cowering all the while, tried to share in his success with a cry of 'We did all right!'

Another shoot-out immediately followed in a garage. This time the two ex-buddies fought side by side and the duel was even sillier, with the gangsters groaning away and Hollywood's two leading macho men upstaging each other by producing larger and larger barrelled pistols, a phallic joke at their expense.

The climax took place in a brothel. Murphy, interrupting one senator's fantasy session, pinched his costume and dressed up as the Wolf in *Red Riding Hood*. Sadly, once Reynolds was in drag, nothing was made of it. Murphy had come to save his kidnapped girlfriend, an heiress, who was playing cards with the gangsters and winning. 'Are you all right?' he had enquired over the phone. 'Hell, no,' she had replied. 'My hair is a mess. I broke two of my fingernails. I don't have my make-up and I'm stuck here with these two ugly, smelly garbage cans.' (She was referring to the gangsters.) The production should have made much more use of Madeline Kahn, who was perfect casting for this dizzy blonde who wore only a fur coat and undies.

Jane Alexander had the Eve Arden role of the wisecracking, unpaid secretary, but without the wisecracks. Richard Roundtree was Murphy's corrupt partner who was playing one big-shot off against another. Roundtree, bowler-hatted, waistcoated, gloved, spatted, was very stylish and looked as if he were about to start tap-dancing at any minute. He met a horrific end, when he was hurled from a fourth-floor window and landed on top of a car. The incident belonged in a different movie. So, too, did that shot of a man, drenched in gasoline, catching light and burning to death.

They succeed all too well in providing an almost offensively clownish waste of time and talent.

Philip Strick, *Observer*

Too often it's like watching a couple of cash-registers upstaging each other.

Alexander Walker, *Standard*

It is hard to know whether this is meant to be a romp or a serious thriller; perhaps because it fails to be either.

Francis Wheen, *New Statesman*

City Heat **– need I say it – is a two-fisted, red-blooded, all-American macho movie with huge hairy balls and plenty good fire-power.**

Mat Snow, *New Musical Express*

Clint Eastwood in
City Heat

148

PALE RIDER

Directed by Clint Eastwood   1985

And I looked and behold a pale horse: and his name that sat on him was Death, and hell followed him.

Revelations 6.8

A small community of poor, independent, hard-working gold prospectors were constantly being harassed by a big mine company that wanted to drive them off their land. The screenplay, a classic confrontation between Good and Evil, paid a nostalgic debt to the Western genre in general and to *Shane* in particular.

Pale Rider had a tremendous opening, the camera alternating between a hard-riding posse and the peaceful mining community, the menace of the riders under-scored on the soundtrack by the thundering hooves of their horses. The riders destroyed everything in their path.

A young girl prayed at the grave of her dog for a miracle and immediately Clint Eastwood appeared out of nowhere, the answer to any maiden's prayer. Since he wore a dog collar, the community presumed he was a man of God and called him Preacher. His Christianity was of the muscular sort and he was as adept at breaking boulders as he was at breaking a man's balls. Mouthing platitudes, he stressed traditional values and delivered a sermon on the need to stand tall against oppression and wanton destruction. Gradually he pulled the community together.

There was a fine performance by Michael Moriarty as the mild-mannered, decent Hull, who lived with his girlfriend, Sarah (Carrie Snodgrass), a widow, and her 15-year-old daughter, Megan (Sydney Penny). Both women

Clint Eastwood in
Pale Rider

Clint Eastwood in
Pale Rider

were attracted to Preacher. He reminded Sarah of the husband who had deserted her. 'Who are you really?' she asked. 'Well, it really doesn't matter, does it?' he replied. Megan wanted to have sex and when he refused, she rode off so that she could be raped and he could come and rescue her in the nick of time.

Hull's character grew as the story progressed. It was he who persuaded the other prospectors to stay in a key speech: 'Gold ain't what we're about. I came here to raise family. This is my home. This is my dream . . . If we sell out now, what price do we put on our dignity next time?'

Eastwood, bringing his subtle command to bear, made the story more mystical, more biblical, more supernatural. Preacher wasn't a preacher; the dog collar was a disguise and he was liable to disappear out of the frame without warning. He was more like a Fourth Horseman of the Apocalypse, resurrected from the dead to save the poor from the rich and to exact his own personal revenge. His gift to the community was to blast the company's mine, buildings and installations.

The bad guys were not slow to recognize his qualities: 'You're a trouble-maker, Preacher, you spell bad cess in letters that stretch from here to Seattle.' The mining company hired Marshal Stockburn (John Russell) to kill him. The Marshal brought along six deputies, professional killers every one of them. In their long raincoats, they looked as if they were modelling clothes for Calvin Klein. (The producers were at pains to point out that the raincoats were actual copies of the 'dusters' men used to wear in the 1870s.) The deputies had no individuality; they were dummies in a shop window and Preacher, in the final shoot-out, dispatched them one by one with ease.

Eastwood had felt the story needed a prior relationship between Stockburn and Preacher. What the relationship had been was never divulged. It was enough to know there was an old score to be settled. Listening to a description, Stockburn felt he knew the man but the man was dead (and the implication was that he had shot him). Face to face, he recognized him instantly: 'YOU! YOU! YOU!' Preacher shot him down and the bullet wounds in the Marshal's back matched the wounds in Preacher's back (which had been seen earlier while he was washing) and they matched them exactly.

Pale Rider, ecologically opportune, had a love for the land the big corporation was blasting away with their hydraulic machinery. The film was shot on location, predominantly in Sun Valley, Idaho, with additional footage in Sonora, California. The scenery, with its russet autumnal plains and snow-capped mountains, was ravishing. The striking photography was by Bruce Surtees, whose dark, sombre interiors caught what it must have been like to live with

only two or three little lamps lighting the whole house.

Mr Eastwood has continued to refine the identity of his Western hero by eliminating virtually every superfluous gesture. He's a master of minimalism. The camera does not reflect vanity. It discovers the mythical character within.

Vincent Canby, *New York Times*

It is difficult to admire Clint Eastwood: the strong, silent manner seems only to camouflage a ham actor, and that wrinkled visage only obscures the essential paucity of his imagination (when he is writer or director).

Peter Ackroyd, *Spectator*

Eastwood acts with his usual half-serious, half-mocking sense of his own flintlike authority and he holds the movie together.

David Denby, *New York Magazine*

The movie is full of recycled mythmaking, but Eastwood goes through the motions like someone exhumed, and as a director he numbs what he borrows.

Pauline Kael, *New Yorker*

Clint Eastwood, Sydney Penny and Michael Moriarty in *Pale Rider*

HEARTBREAK RIDGE

Directed by Clint Eastwood   1986

Every effort was made to ensure *Heartbreak Ridge* was as accurate and as representative of the United States Marine Corps as possible. The production was made with their technical assistance. However, when the powers-that-be saw the finished product, they withdrew their support, finding the brutality, violence and foul language non-productive.

The film began with black and white news-reel footage from Korea. Pictures of wounded and dead soldiers were not quite what the Marine Corps had had in mind as a recruiting advertisement. They would have preferred something along the lines of *Top Guns* (though, presumably, not if they had learned of Quentin Tarantino's discovery of a gay subtext). They objected to the sergeant's habit of addressing the recruits as 'ladies', 'missies', 'queer-bait', and telling them that he 'didn't want to take long, lingering showers with them'.

The movie was an elegy for a Marine lifer, an old-timer with an excellent military record and a chestful of medals to confirm it. Tough, honest and gung-ho, he had fought with valour in Vietnam and won a Congressional Medal of Honour at Heartbreak Ridge, Korea. The film's title referred not only to the battle but also to the contemporary turning point in his life when his career was nearing its mandatory end.

Sergeant Tom Highway, bull-necked, square-headed, hair close-cropped, had a will of iron and he could out-drink, out-brawl and out-swear anybody. He knew how to deal quickly and efficiently with a hulking prison lout. (The scene recalled a similar exchange in *Escape from Alcatraz*.) He was not amused when a gay

Clint Eastwood and platoon train in *Heartbreak Ridge*

154

Clint Eastwood in
Heartbreak Ridge

Clint Eastwood and
Mario Van Peebles in
Heartbreak Ridge

soldier on a bus gave him the eye; but then, he had only himself to blame, since he was reading a woman's magazine at the time.

Highway didn't know where he was going. He had nowhere to go; the army was his life. Unable to face the future, he decided to make it up with his ex-wife (Marsha Mason) and read women's magazines to try to find out why their marriage had failed. (Did we mutually nurture each other? he asked himself. Did we communicate in a meaningful way in our relationship? he wondered. The screenplay parodied the language of such magazines.) The marriage had failed because of his thoughtlessness, his machismo and the job itself. Marines and marriage, as far as his ex-wife was concerned, were incompatible.

The psychological traumas had warped his character. The scars run deep, said the poster. The outer wounds were visible on his neck and forehead. The leather skin was stretched like scar tissue and the voice was gravel-hoarse from drinking and barking. Eastwood, not afraid to look old and ugly, was very convinc-

ing as an NCO. The strength of the performance was the sense of failure beneath the aggressive macho posturing.

Highway went back to his old combat unit to transform raw recruits into 'lifetakers and heartbreakers'. His training was rigorous ('I understand a lot of body bags get filled if I don't do my job') and his discipline was relentless ('We may have lost the wars, but we won the battles. I'm not going to lose the next one because my men are not ready').

The platoon was a rebellious, insubordinate and recalcitrant lot and they did not hide their contempt for authority. Used to a lazy life, they resented and hated Highway until he had knocked them into shape. Then, of course, he won their loyalty. Mario Van Peebles had the most showy role of all the recruits, playing a cocky, backchatting rapper and rock singer, a self-proclaimed Ayatollah of Rock 'n' Roll. The exuberant Van Peebles sang his own songs, wore a T-shirt with the legend 'I'm sexy' on it and provided the humour.

Highway (as you would expect in a Clint Eastwood movie) was in conflict with his inefficient superiors. His lieutenant was a naïve wimp straight out of college. His major (Everett McGill, well cast) was a bureaucratic martinet with no experience of combat. 'I asked for marines,' the major observed. 'The Division sent me relics. You're an anachronism. Characters like you ought to be in a case that reads "break glass only in the event of war".' Highway, constantly usurping the major's authority, deviated from his training programme and, as is the way in American war movies, the two men, eventually, had a hand-to-hand fight, egged on by the other ranks.

Heartbreak Ridge stayed in the camp right until the very end, when the men were flown out to Grenada for a bit of jingoistic action, and Highway, inevitably going against the major's orders, led his platoon to victory, rescuing American citizens from their Cuban captors. The fact that he shot the enemy in the back and then smoked his cigar didn't go down too well with the Marines.

As director, Eastwood revitalizes old clichés, and as an actor he gives Highway considerable depth and complexity. He is the oldest character Eastwood has played, and he makes him a wonderfully tough, amusing, humane and vulnerable man.

Philip French, *Observer*

As the gritty, raspy-voiced sergeant, Mr Eastwood's performance is one of the richest he's ever given. It's funny, laid-back, seemingly effortless, the sort that separates actors who are run-of-the-mill from those who have earned the right to be identified as stars.

Vincent Canby, *Time*

It would take a board of inquiry made up of gods to determine whether this picture is more offensive aesthetically, psychologically, morally or politically.

Pauline Kael, *New Yorker*

The incessant pornographic talk, its obsessional fear of male femininity, is so homophobic as to be, in spite of itself, extremely camp. Eastwood may find his film has an admiring audience that he never intended to impress.

William Green, *Today Sunday*

Charmless advertisement for testosterone imperialism.

Adam Mars-Jones, *Independent*

BIRD

Directed by Clint Eastwood   1988

The picture is kind of constructed like a jazz tune. It asks the audience to listen carefully. Otherwise they may miss elements of it, much like a Charles Parker solo.

Clint Eastwood,
quoted by Derek Malcolm, *Guardian*

'Bird' was the nickname of Charlie Parker, the great bebop saxophone player who revolutionized the way everyone played the saxophone. The movie, dedicated to musicians everywhere, was both a lament for the man and a homage to his music.

Clint Eastwood, who had been a jazz aficionado nearly all his life, had seen Parker in 1945 in Oakland, California, when he was a teenager. In attempting to create a narrative and visual equivalent to Parker's complicated music, he shuffled time, jumping back and forth in time. The multiple flashbacks made it difficult for the average audience to follow. The soundtrack paralleled the neurotic speed of uptake in bebop itself, blending the original solos with fresh back-ups. The combination of the new, the old and the refurbished material worried the purists. The technical skill with which it was done won an award for sound recording at the Cannes Film Festival.

Jack N. Green's lighting was atmospheric. *Bird* had the feel of a downbeat *film noir*. It was always night-time and it seemed to be always raining; but in creating the dark, smoky world of the nightclubs, it was often difficult to see what was going on, so swallowed up were the black actors in the darkness and shadow. As for the pretty studio street, with its period cars, it looked like a setting more appropriate for a period musical.

Clint Eastwood directs
Samuel E. Wright and
Forest Whitaker in *Bird*

159

Forest Whitaker and
Diane Venora in *Bird*

'There are no second acts in American lives,' wrote F. Scott Fitzgerald. Bird (Forest Whitaker, very impressive), musical genius, womanizer, heroin addict, had a messy, complicated life and an infinite capacity for causing havoc. Dizzy Gillespie (Samuel E. Wright), unlike Parker, always made a point of arriving on time and he did so because he didn't want to give white people the pleasure of having their beliefs that 'the nigger was unreliable' confirmed.

Joel Oliansky's often harrowing screenplay ignored Parker's childhood, formative years and marriages to concentrate, in a collage of scenes and impressions, on his declining career and his love for the protective and stoical Chan Richardson (Diane Venora, also very impressive), whom he constantly let down. Perhaps the most moving moment was his reaction to the death of his daughter when, tearfully and drunkenly, he sent telegram after telegram to her. There was a rare moment of joy in the seemingly never-ending misery, when he arrived on horseback to woo Chan. Bird ended up in an asylum, when what he really needed was medical treatment, not psychology. He

died of drugs and alcohol at the age of 34. The doctor, examining the dead body, thought he was about 65.

There were two recurring images: a doctor showing him a corpse and a flying cymbal, a memory of the occasion, when in mid-solo at Kansas City Jazz Club, he had been humiliated by drummer J. Jones untying his cymbal and throwing it on to the floor.

Parker's relationship with the white trumpet player, Red Rodney (Michael Zelniker), was historically interesting and there was a fascinating sequence where, in order to be able to play in the Deep South, Rodney had to be passed off as an albino.

Bird won the Golden Globe award and Forest Whitaker won the best actor award at the Cannes Film festival.

At last American cinema has done black music proud. Unforgettable.

Brian Case, *Time Out*

This is a hugely ambitious piece of film-making and further proof that Eastwood stands alongside Woody Allen in the vanguard of those pushing the American cinema ahead.

Philip French, *Observer*

It invites us to experience the redeeming grace of his music. And with its passionate craft it proclaims that Eastwood is a major American director.

Richard Schickel, *Time*

It's an honourable and skilful piece of work, the most complicated of all Eastwood's ventures as director and the most mature.

Derek Malcolm, *Guardian*

THE DEAD POOL

Directed by Buddy Van Horn   1988

The Dead Pool raised questions about what audiences should be allowed to see on their screens and who was to decide what was harmful. Harry Callahan, strongly critical of the media, didn't like the way television intruded into people's grief and berated a film crew: 'You're only interested in death and mayhem.' It was ironic that Callahan of all people should criticize the media for doing what the 'Dirty Harry' films had been doing for years. He smashed a camera. The television company brought a law suit. His superior wanted to take him off the streets. He threatened to resign. Nothing new.

The reporter (Patricia Clarkson, who looked a bit like Sondra Locke) admitted later that she had made an error of judgement and they became good friends. Easily the most inter-esting scene they shared was the one in which they failed to talk a man out of suicide. Wanting his 15 minutes of fame, he decided to get on the 6 o'clock news by setting himself on fire in front of a television camera.

The Dead Pool was a hit list, a ghoulish game instigated by a paranoid film director, a cine-pseud, who made cheap, schlock horror movies at the back of a meat factory. His crew took bets on who they thought was the next person most likely to die. They fixed on celebrities who weren't going to make it because they were either old or sick or in a high-risk profession. Somebody had got hold of the list and was working their way through it. A rock star was murdered. A talk-show host was murdered. A production assistant was murdered. A female film critic was murdered. (It wasn't very difficult to guess which critics the movie had in mind.) Callahan was also on the list. He had

just put a major crime figure in prison and was the hero of the hour, the target of the media, hired guns and lunatics.

The film director (Liam Neeson) was a prime suspect; but it was obvious somebody was impersonating him and trying to frame him. The director thought it could be anybody: his agent, the producers of his last film, the crew, the public, the critics. 'It's jealousy,' he whined. 'They envy my talent. They want to destroy it.' Neeson, wearing a ponytail and an earring, was not good and his accent a camp caricature. 'Let me tell you something,' he said. 'People are fascinated by death and violence. That is why my films make money. They are an escape, a vicarious release of fear. Nobody takes my film or the game seriously.'

The murderer was mentally ill and the game had become an obsession. The psychiatrist (who had let him out of an institution) said that he was someone whose sense of self-hatred was so extreme that he no longer had a self but substituted the identity of a celebrity for his own. He had stolen the director's identity.

There were occasional jokes at the expense of the crime genre and the audience, too. The first was when two guys asked Callahan for his autograph and he mistook them for hit men. The second was when he was out jogging and was being followed by two men in car, who turned out to be bodyguards sent by the imprisoned crime lord to protect him.

The streets of San Francisco are always good for a car chase. The high spot, though not nearly exciting enough, or funny enough, and far too long, was a parody of *Bullitt*. Callahan was chased by a remote-controlled dinky toy car which was wired with explosives.

Clint Eastwood and
Patricia Clarkson in
The Dead Pool

The psychopath kidnapped the reporter; no psychopath worthy of the name ever fails to kidnap the hero's girlfriend in the last reel. The final shoot-out took place in the docks, where Callahan, finally, managed to nail the villain with a harpoon, pinning him to the wall. The pay-off line was very James Bond: 'He's hanging out back there,' he said to the police, who, as usual, only arrived when it was all over.

Clint Eastwood's shoot-first cop, in the fifth of the series, is so shop-soiled with cliché that it would need a whole laundry of new ideas to freshen him up.

Tom Hutchinson, *Mail on Sunday*

One suspects that Eastwood, aware of passing time, has taken to quiet mockery of role and genre, to save anyone else the trouble.

Shaun Usher, *Daily Mail*

The word 'dead' in the title is brutally appropriate.

Derek Malcolm, *Guardian*

Perhaps Dirty Harry should retire and go into local politics.

Douglas Young, *Scotsman Weekend*

Clint Eastwood in
The Dead Pool

PINK CADILLAC

Directed by Buddy Van Horn   1989

Tommy Nowak: Have you seen a blonde in a
pink Cadillac?
Garage Attendant: Only in my dreams.

Clint Eastwood was cast as Tommy Nowak, a
skip-tracer, hired by bail bondsmen. ('That's
my job,' he said. 'Track 'em and snatch 'em.')
The role afforded him opportunities for funny
disguises while making comic arrests. He
played a disc jockey, a chauffeur, a red-nosed
clown at a rodeo and a moustached guy in a
gold lamé jacket. His most amusing disguise
was his dumbo redneck, chewing and spitting
baccy. 'Pretty thin line between what you do
and some outlaws do,' remarked one lawyer.
'Maybe a thin line, but it isn't invisible,'
Nowak retorted.

Bernadette Peters was cast as Lou Ann
McGuinn, a young mother with an eight-
month-old baby and married to a dim-witted
and weak-willed member of The Birthright
Organization, which was run by pony-tailed
Alex (Michael Des Barres), a vicious neo-
fascist. His followers were small-time thieves,
junkies, wife-beaters, drifters and psychos, and
they spent their days shooting targets with
automatic weapons at their arsenal in the
forest. They were so moronic, they could have
joined The Black Widows bike gang in *Every
Which Way But Loose* and few people would
have noticed the difference.

Lou Ann, fed up with her husband (Timothy
Carhart), went off with his Cadillac, his prize
possession, and, inadvertently, a quarter of a
million dollars, the prize possession of The
Birthright Organization which they had just
stolen from a bank and had told her was
counterfeit money. She was the palest thing,

Clint Eastwood and
Bernadette Peters in
Pink Cadillac

with cupid-bowed lips, and at one point she
was driving down the road with the notes
flying out of the back of the car, just like any
heroine in a Frank Capra comedy. 'I'm through
taking shit from men,' she confided to Nowak.
'That's one thing we have in common,' he
replied. 'I'm through taking shit from men.'
They shared a room in a hotel and, a bit later,
they shared a bed in a motel. 'I've got a firm
policy on gun control,' he said. 'If there's a gun
around, I want to be the person controlling it.'

The innuendo wasn't bad ('I don't mean to
interfere with your marriage, but it's dangerous
messing around with a man's vehicles') and
just in case audiences missed the innuendo
first time round, it was repeated throughout the
movie. There was also a gratuitous and not
original exchange between a flasher and Lou
Ann. 'What do you think?' asked the flasher. 'It
looks like a penis,' she replied, 'only smaller.'
The screenplay should have been tighter, and
more could have made of the bungled arrest in
a crowded casino and the sequence where the
couple were trapped in a car-wash and nearly
blown up by a bomb in a baby doll.

John Dennis Johnston,
Timothy Carhart,
Bernadette Peters
and Clint Eastwood in
Pink Cadillac

The trouble with Eastwood's role was that it was totally impossible to believe that Nowak would ever have been a pushover for such a silly woman as Lou Ann and that he would have thrown in his job for her. The trouble with Peters's role was that the development of her character was equally unconvincing. The two were meant to have been brought closer by having been shooting together, but they remained a charmless, unlikely partnership and the sexual ding-dong was nil.

There was an over-the-top comic turn by Geoffrey Lewis as a zany, mangy, spaced-out guy who forged identification papers, which led to an unpleasant scene when The Birthright Organization beat him up and trashed his property, setting the place alight and leaving him to burn inside.

The climax took place in the forest. 'I am going to have to ask you, are you an organ donor, Alex?' asked Nowak, with a gun to Alex's head, giving a very good imitation of Dirty Harry. In the final chase, he and Lou Ann were so outnumbered and so out-gunned that the whole thing became farcical. Cars were

being driven off the road, cars were being driven into shacks, cars were nosediving into rivers, cars were overturning and cars were falling to bits. Bullets were flying, Eastwood was driving, Peters was screaming, the baby was crying and nobody was wearing seat-belts. The stunt men had a great time.

The soundtrack, top-heavy with country tunes, was aimed at a young audience. 'We can't see round the bend,' sang one group, 'we never know where the road might end, we just go anywhere.' Just like *Pink Cadillac*. Understandably, Eastwood's heart didn't seem to be in it.

The film gives us no reason to think these two people are even slightly attracted to each other. Mr Eastwood and Ms Peters might as well have been filmed separately and spliced together.

Caryn James, *New York Times*

I just wish this vehicle had some juice.

Georgia Brown, *Village Voice*

The 1990s

Clint Eastwood in
A Perfect World

WHITE HUNTER, BLACK HEART

Directed by Clint Eastwood   1990

It is not about the making of The African Queen. *It is not about Bogart and Hepburn and Bacall. It's about a film director with a powerful obsession that brushed everyone and everything else aside – and the deadly cost of that obsession.*

Peter Viertel

White Hunter, Black Heart was a portrait of the legendary film director John Huston, based on Peter Viertel's *roman à clef*, published in 1953, which gave a fictional account of his experiences while working on the script of *The African Queen* on location in Uganda and the Belgian Congo in 1950. The screenplay had been kicking around for 30 years and there had been any number of options taken on it before Clint Eastwood decided to do it.

John Wilson (as Huston was called in the film) was an ogre, a pain in the arse, an unreasonable, bloody-minded, unprofessional, selfish bastard, who continually violated the unwritten laws of the motion-picture business, yet had the magic, almost divine ability to land on his feet. His creative talent was never in any doubt. A professional smile always at the ready, he remained a mass of contradictions. On the one hand, he had a charismatic charm, wit and intelligence; on the other, a boorish, reckless, swaggering megalomania. 'We are gods,' he said, 'lousy little gods, who control the lives of the people we create, deciding whether they have the right to live', and he wasn't just talking about the characters in the screenplay.

Wilson was very clear about his priorities. He had got a fever; it was like a passion, a demon, and he wouldn't be all right until he had killed an elephant. He saw the film as an all-expenses-paid safari. Broke himself (he owed $300,000), he was quite willing to let the whole movie go down the drain and bankrupt the company. He didn't give a damn. 'You're either crazy or the most egocentric, irresponsible son of a bitch that I've ever met,' said Peter Verrill (the Peter Viertel role, played by Jeff Fahey).

Wilson was as much an endangered species as the bull elephant he wanted to kill. When the producer insisted the rapids sequence was too dangerous and ordered it to be cut from the film, his immediate response was to get into a tacky boat and shoot the rapids. 'Do you know why I agreed to work with him?' he asked Verrill rhetorically. 'Because it was the wrong thing to do.'

In England, dressed in jodhpurs, he adopted a patronizing English accent and rode with the hounds, a caricature of an English lord. In Africa, he followed in the footsteps of Ernest Hemingway and acted the great white hunter. His producer longed for him to drop both roles and become a film director again.

There were two set-pieces. The first, very contrived and theatrical, was with a woman (Mel Martin) Wilson had hoped to bed, but she proved so anti-Semitic that he changed his mind. 'You, my dear, are the ugliest, goddamn bitch I've ever dined with.' The second, immediately following, was with the racist hotel manager (Clive Mantle) and ended in fisticuffs, with him (contrary to the audience's expectations) rather than the manager getting beaten up. It might have been more of a moral victory had he not been drunk at the time.

Wilson would come to the aid of the underdog, yet he could be high-handed, condescend-

George Dzundza and Clint Eastwood in *White Hunter, Black Heart*

168

ing, exploitative and cruel to the people closest to him, insulting scriptwriter, producer, money men, unit manager and secretary. He needed constantly to assert himself; he was always spoiling for a fight, sneering at everybody else's lack of manliness. Even his jokes were sadistic. A nerve-racking flight with an incompetent pilot (droopy-drawers Timothy Spall) turned out to have been arranged merely to give Verrill a fright. The picture was filmed in Zimbabwe and the flight was really an excuse for a gratuitous aerial shot of the Victoria Falls, yet little was made of the local footage elsewhere.

When the stars, Humphrey Bogart and Katharine Hepburn (played by lookalikes Richard Vanstone and Marisa Berenson) finally arrived in Africa, Wilson laid on a slap-up dinner and then proceeded to humiliate the producer in front of everybody. His humiliation was abetted by a scurrying monkey tearing up the one and only script. (George Dzundza was well cast as the exasperated butt for Wilson's contempt.) There were also major conflicts between director and scriptwriter over the screenplay. Wilson wanted to blow up the ship and kill everybody. Verrill preferred a happy ending. 'Why are you so concerned about the damn audience?' demanded Wilson. 'Because we're in show business!' replied Verrill.

Right at the very end, Wilson admitted, 'You were right, Pete, the ending's all wrong.' It was an ironic and deliberately ambiguous line, referring both to the end of the film they were about to shoot and to the end of *White Hunter, Black Heart* itself. *The African Queen*, one of Huston's most popular films, had ended happily on a silly coda and had been a huge success; *White Hunter, Black Heart*, already far

too off-beat a subject for Eastwood's regular fans, ended on a downbeat note and was a box-office failure.

The 60-year-old Clint Eastwood, playing the 45-year-old John Huston, did not resort to glib impersonation. His incarnation was rather an evocation of the man, his speech, mannerisms, clothes, cigars. There were those who found the performance a bit too laid-back, too light, vocally and physically, to be convincing; yet Wilson's comments on screenwriting could easily have been Eastwood's own credo: 'Things are always good if they are left simple. Don't complicate, you'll be wasting your time.' (Eastwood's films never get bogged down in a subplot.) 'You can't let 85 million popcorn-eaters pull you this way and that. To write a movie you have to forget anyone is going to see it.' (Maybe he was thinking of two of his favourite pictures, *Bronco Billy* and *Honkytonk Man*?)

Wilson had a key scene with the unit manager (Alun Armstrong), who was in charge of the budget. The manager was an odious, sour little man, a spy for head office, on the bottle and invariably rude to the natives. Wilson turned on him for using 'Hollywood' as a pejorative term: 'People say "Hollywood" when they want to insult you. They are not talking about the people who work and try to

Boy Mathias Chuma and Clint Eastwood in White Hunter, Black Heart

Clint Eastwood in White Hunter, Black Heart

do something worthwhile. They are talking about the whores – whores who sell words and ideas and melodies. I know what I'm talking about because I have done a lot of hustling in my time – a hell of a lot more than I'd like to admit.' (Was he, perhaps, thinking of *The Dead Pool* and *Pink Cadillac*?)

There were intellectual debates between Wilson and Verrill about the elephant. Verrill thought it a crime to kill one of the rarest and most noble creatures to roam the earth. Wilson tried, unsuccessfully, to explain himself: 'It's not a crime to kill an elephant. It's bigger than that. It's a sin to kill an elephant. You understand that. It's the only sin you can buy a licence for and go out and commit. That's why I want to do it before I do anything else in the world. Do you understand me? Of course, you do not. I don't understand myself.'

The climax was brilliantly handled and deeply moving. Wilson, finally, came face to face with the elephant. (The casting people had more difficulty casting the elephant than any other role; in the event, the elephant was superb.) Man and beast were seen in enormous close-ups, a confrontation which some likened to Captain Ahab's with Moby Dick. (Huston had filmed the Herman Melville classic in 1956.) Wilson faltered, unable to pull the trigger. In the novel he killed the elephant. Here the elephant backed off, only immediately to turn round and charge, seemingly to protect a baby elephant. The native guide (Boy Mathias Chuma) tried to intervene and was thrown, mauled and killed, the swirling camera emphasizing the horror.

The final scene of all, back on the set, was equally well-handled, intercutting between the grief-stricken villagers and the film company. Wilson asked what the native drumbeats meant and was told that they meant bad news and that they always began with the same words: white hunter, black heart. He sat there, slumped in his director's chair, deeply shaken, a gaunt, silent, numbed, sick figure. The tragic outcome of his folly and arrogance had finally cut him down to size. He was filled with shame, self-hatred and remorse. The actors, the producer and the crew waited for him to give the signal to start. It was a long, long wait before he said, very softly, 'Action!' Eastwood was excellent.

White Hunter, Black Heart is an honourable piece of work because it refuses to remain the sort of film that audiences will expect.

Anthony Lane, *Independent on Sunday*

Eastwood can't decide whether to impersonate the great man or play it light and easy. He loses himself somewhere between the two, appearing both ludicrous and wooden.

Angus Wolfe Murray, *Scotsman Weekend*

Eastwood's portrait of the egotistical Huston is by far his best performance to date.

Adrian Turner, *Sunday Correspondent*

Eastwood's menopausal machismo nightmare is strained – lacking the tension, rigorous thought and visceral power of his best work.

Gavin Martin, *New Musical Express*

After this movie, not even Clint Eastwood's harshest judge could deny him his rightful place in the top echelons of actors and directors.

Richard Blaine, *Today*

THE ROOKIE

Directed by Clint Eastwood   1990

The Rookie, a story of a veteran cop and his wet-behind-the-ears partner, was a 'Dirty Harry' film in all but name. They were members of the Grand Theft Auto Division of the Los Angeles Police Department looking into a $2 million raid.

Clint Eastwood may have got top billing but, as the title suggested, he was playing a supporting role to the rookie. He was cast as Nick Pulovski, a sour, cynical, caustic cop who smoked cigars. (The running gag was that he never had a light.) Obsessed with avenging the murder of his partner, he patronized the rookie. Eastwood was his usual confrontational, aggressive self. The dialogue, full of cliché-ridden banalities, was often unintentionally funny.

Charlie Sheen played the rookie, David Ackerman, a poor-little-rich-boy who had joined the force two years previously to spite his parents. ('Where were you when I was in pain? You were never there for me, Dad.'). He had also joined to try to expiate guilty feelings about the death of his brother in an accident for which he had been partly to blame. His father said he needed to forgive himself. The rookie needed to forgive himself even more when, unable to kill the villainess, he dithered and Pulovski was kidnapped. 'Amateur!' she screamed, shooting him. He smashed his head against a mirror until the mirror cracked, because that is what some movie actors do when they want to signal their frustration.

Ackerman became determined to prove his manhood to his colleagues and his girlfriend. 'I'm through making mistakes,' he declared. 'It's time for me to stop being scared and other people to start.' He took off his suit, put on a

Charlie Sheen and Clint Eastwood in *The Rookie*

denim jacket and went back to the bikers' bar (where earlier he had been beaten up) and smashed up the joint, single-handedly, and then set it alight. He walked out of the burning building, no longer 'a damned yellow rookie', no longer 'a fresh-faced punk', but a man, and just in case cinemagoers hadn't noticed what a man the rookie had become, he threw away his motorcycle helmet, got on his bike and drove through his front door to save his girlfriend from being murdered. He then drove off to rescue his partner. Sheen, who managed to be both chubby and wooden, was an unlikely tough guy.

The villains were a way-over-the-top couple. There was Strom, a ruthless, big-time German thief, played by South American actor Raul Julia who sported a dreadful accent and a

Sonia Braga and
Clint Eastwood in
The Rookie

comic moustache. His partner and lover (Sonia Braga), a scantily clad *femme fatale*, was equally absurd. She behaved as if she were in a James Bond movie and gave Pulovski a good licking. 'Are you man? Are you any different?' she asked, ripping open his shirt and playing with a razor blade. 'You better be, because I hate anything useless. When something is no good to me, I cut it off and throw it away.' The armchair bondage and fellatio were recorded on banks of television screens. Rape was not unusual in an Eastwood movie, but this was the first time that he was the one being raped. While he was being abused, the TV networks were showing an old monster movie and a very large black spider was briefly observed on the screen. This was a private joke, which may have been missed. The movie was *Tarantula*, one of the very first movies Eastwood had made. He was the pilot who had bombed the tarantula.

There was a good moment when he took a small-time crook and his car for a ride in a wrecking yard and there was also a good joke, badly handled, when he and Ackerman made a surprise entrance, stepping out of a gambling casino's safe. The highlights were two action sequences. The first, excellently edited by Joel Cox, came right at the beginning, providing the fans with what they had come to see. Pulovski was in full pursuit of Strom, who was making his escape in a double-decker transporter loaded with Porsches, Jaguars and Mercedes. A member of the gang (Marco Rodriguez, with a good pockmarked villain's face) released three automobiles on to the motorway, causing mayhem. He dodged the crashing cars and drove on to the carrier. The gang member then released the whole trailer, spewing cars all over the place in a tremendous pile-up. Bill Young's precision-driving team stole all the notices.

The stunt work was equally impressive when Pulovski and Ackerman were making their escape from the top floor of a warehouse by driving through a floor-to-ceiling window as the building detonated. They landed on the roof of another building, fell through the skylight into a warehouse and drove straight to San Jose International Airport, where a private jet tried to run them down as they raced across the fields. Hands up all those who have seen Alfred Hitchcock's *North by Northwest*. The homage to Hitchcock had been much better expressed earlier, in a dry-cleaning shop, when a garrotted corpse was discovered hanging among the laundry on a spinning carousel.

Pulovski and Ackerman entered the main building via the luggage hold – a nice idea which would have been even better had it been

more imaginatively and wittily stage-managed. While chasing round the crowded airport, full of screaming, ducking extras pretending to be passengers, Ackerman managed to save his partner from being killed by shooting both villains dead. 'Amateur!' he screamed. The two wounded men sat together, sporting their bloody gashes, and they would have smoked a post-coital cigar had they had a light.

In an unlikely and glib coda, the veteran cop had been kicked upstairs and was doing a desk job and the rookie had stepped into his shoes. *The Rookie* was for diehard fans only.

While learning how to please arthouse audiences, Clint Eastwood has forgotten how to make popular entertainment.

Philip French, *Observer*

This is a shameless exercise in quickie production money-making that relies on the idea that audiences won't notice the joins if there is enough crash, bang, wallop.

Sue Heal, *Today*

It's sad to watch a superstar going through the motions.

Shaun Usher, *Daily Mail*

I enjoyed every minute. There is no star like an old star.

Nigel Andrews, *Financial Times*

Clint Eastwood and Raul Julia in *The Rookie*

UNFORGIVEN

Directed by Clint Eastwood   1992

I thought it was very timely to do a film where violence not only can be painful, but has consequences for the perpetrators as well as the victims. Usually in Westerns violence is glorified and romanticized. We demythicize it.

Clint Eastwood,
quoted by John Hiscock, *Daily Telegraph*

Unforgiven (dedicated to Eastwood's mentors, Sergio Leone and Don Siegel) was an elegiac Western set in 1880, the year of President Garfield's assassination. The film (originally called *The Cat Whore Killings*) opened with violence in the local brothel in the ramshackle town of Big Whiskey in Wyoming. One of the girls (Anna Thomson), new to the job, dared to laugh at her customer's little pecker and had her face slashed. The brothel owner, who treated the girls as his property, demanded compensation, not for them but for himself. The sheriff fined the cowboys seven ponies. The whores, who had expected a whipping at the very least, were outraged and, led by Strawberry Alice (Frances Fisher), the whorehouse madam, offered $1,000 reward to anybody who killed the men.

William Munny (Clint Eastwood), 'a known thief and murderer, a man of notoriously vicious and intemperate disposition', had been cured of his wickedness by his wife. Totally reformed, he was a sensitive, single parent, looking after two young children and trying, unsuccessfully, to eke out a living on a broken-down pig farm. His wife had died at 29 of smallpox, three years before the story began, but her presence was felt throughout the film. Ever faithful to her memory, the last thing he wanted to do was resume his former trade, so

when a young bounty hunter (Jaimz Woolvett) asked him to be his partner, he turned him down. However, his destitution, and the need to feed his children, forced him to change his mind and he invited his former partner, Ned Logan (Morgan Freeman), also an old man and retired, to join him.

The bounty hunter, who called himself the Schofield Kid, was disappointed to find that Munny wasn't the mean, cold, crazy, no-good-son-of-a-bitch killer of legend that he had expected to see. The Kid was, literally and symbolically, a short-sighted youth. (His naïvety and hero-worshipping brought back memories of the role Timothy Bottoms had played in *The Outlaw Josey Wales*.)

The Sheriff (Gene Hackman) was a smiling fascist who wanted law and order and did what he thought best for the community; and what he did best was punch and kick a man when he was down. When English Bob (Richard Harris),

a veteran gunfighter, arrived in town, he immediately disarmed him and then, as a warning to all other bounty hunters, he beat the living daylights out of him and put him and his accompanying biographer in jail.

The sheriff gave the biographer, a dime novelist (a comic character played by Saul Rubinek), a true account of Bob's manly exploits and the scene afforded opportunities for satire at the expense of the heroes and legends of the West. The sheriff also enjoyed a little game, giving the Duke (or The Duck, as he preferred to call him) a chance to kill him, which the Duke made the mistake of not taking. The cowardly biographer quickly changed his allegiance.

There was an excellent scene when Munny, sick and feverish, was sitting all by himself in the saloon while his partners were upstairs humping the whores. Surrounded by the sheriff and his deputies, he was asked for his weapons and, when he declined to give them up, he, too, was given a vicious beating. He ended up crawling out on all fours. Eastwood, unshaven, deeply scarred, didn't just look old; he looked as if he were at death's door.

The killing of the first cowboy (a nice lad, not guilty, except by association with his partner) was played for full horror. Ned couldn't bring himself to kill him. The Schofield Kid couldn't see him to kill him. So, it was left to Munny to shoot him. The boy bled to death in a gully. Ned no longer had the stomach and returned home, only to be captured by a posse and whipped to death by the Sheriff. His body was placed in an open coffin outside the saloon with a placard: 'This is what happens to assassins around here.'

The killing of the second cowboy (the fat slob who had actually done the slashing) was carried out by the Schofield Kid while the man was sitting in the privy. The Kid, who had pretended to have killed five men (not that anybody had believed him), found out what it was really like to kill. 'I guess he had it comin',' he said in a pathetic attempt at bravado. 'We all have it comin',' said Munny. The Kid was shattered: 'It don't seem real. How he can never breathe again, how he's dead, all on account of pulling a trigger. I'm going to kill nobody no more. I ain't like you, Will.'

Eastwood, who had hung on to the script, waiting some seven or eight years until he felt he was old enough to play Munny, liked the morality of the story: 'This is the first story I have ever come across where the outlaw had a conscience about what he was doing.'

The horror of the past and its killings continued to haunt Munny to the very end: 'It's a

Clint Eastwood and Anna Thomson in *Unforgiven*

hell of a thing killing a man, taking away all he got and all he's ever going to have.' But goaded by Ned's murder, he yielded to that past and came back to avenge his death. Making his entrance to a clap of thunder, he was transformed into a High Plains Drifter, a Pale Rider, a Man With No Name. He killed the unarmed saloon owner ('He should have armed himself!'), the sheriff and his three deputies, the latter all decent men. 'I have always been lucky when it comes to killing folks,' he said.

The scene may have been good for Eastwood's fans, but it was tragic for Munny, a moral defeat. When the sheriff (the last man to die) said he would see him in hell, it was as if Munny had already been there and was on his way back. He rode out, threatening to return and kill every one of them. He never did come back, though. He moved on to San Francisco and – this was an unexpected, ironic touch – prospered in dry goods.

Clint Eastwood and
Jaimz Woolvett in
Unforgiven

Unforgiven, hard-bitten, hard-edged and highly dramatic, was a brooding and sombre work, its dark tones complemented by photographer Jack Green's sombre and bleak images. (It rained practically all the time.) There was superb location work in Alberta and California.

Unforgiven is Clint Eastwood's masterpiece.

It's Eastwood's best movie and the best Western by anybody in over twenty years.

USA Today

It is a grim picture, lightened by fine acting, beautiful photography, and, most of all, subversively mordant irony.

Stephen Amedon, *Financial Times*

He inhabits the genre like no other contemporary actor.

Hugo Davenport, *Daily Telegraph*

With his new film, *Unforgiven*, Eastwood comes close to pulling a wholly successful modern Western out of the hat. Only the last reel stands in the way of it attaining classic status.

Adam Mars-Jones, *Independent*

Eastwood's stands alone in his commitment to directing and starring in Westerns. *Unforgiven* won't revive the genre, but it will keep the flame alive until the next talent keen to use the country's mythology can put the Western to his uses.

Chris Peachment, *Sunday Times*

If there is anything I learned from Don Siegel, it's to know what you want to shoot and to know what you're seeing when you see it.

Clint Eastwood

IN THE LINE OF FIRE

Directed by Wolfgang Petersen   1993

In the Line of Fire was a first-rate thriller about a bid to assassinate the President of the United States. The President gets 14,000 such threats a year. Clint Eastwood was cast as Frank Horrigan, an elderly undercover agent who volunteered to be attached to the White House to protect him. The big question was, had he got the guts to take the bullet? He was still haunted by his failure 30 years previously to halt the fatal bullets that had killed President Kennedy in Dallas. Had it been cowardice? Or slow reflexes due to a hangover? Could he, this time, save the present incumbent, who was in the middle of a campaign seeking re-election and trailing badly in the polls?

There were already 229 people protecting the President. Was he worth dying for? The answer was almost certainly not, but Horrigan was protecting the office rather than the man. Certainly, he did not feel the allegiance he had felt for JFK. Horrigan, a man of integrity and a patriot, was there to uphold the moral code and, indeed, in order to protect JFK's dignity he had once (very patriotically) pretended that Kennedy's girlfriend, caught in the White House, had been his girlfriend and taken the rap.

Horrigan, who worked by intuition and psychological insight rather than by technology, was described by the backbiters as 'a borderline burnt-out with questionable sociable skills', and, more simply, as a 'dinosaur' and 'too old for this shit'. At 63, it was true he was no longer a young man. The face, worn and overwrought, was deeply fissured and the husky voice was huskier than ever. During a motorcade, he was seen running by the side of the President's car, puffing and coughing away. There were constant references to his age and

lots of self-deprecating jokes, as if the actor wanted to get in there first before anybody else did. When Horrigan said, not without irony, 'You're looking at a living legend', Eastwood could well have been talking about himself.

Though Horrigan was not Dirty Harry, his Dirty Harry credentials were immediately established by his abrasive and confrontational manner with colleagues, and especially in the opening sequence, when he was busting a gang of counterfeiters and put the life of his partner (Dylan McDermott) horribly at risk; and, sure enough, his partner went the way of all Harry's partners. McDermott (in a much more developed part than usual) was very good.

Mitch Leary, the assassin, called himself Booth after the famous actor-assassin who had murdered Abraham Lincoln. He was a master of disguise, constantly changing his appearance and character while dogging Horrigan's footsteps. It was a very long time before his face was seen.

John Malkovich had a sinister calmness which was liable to give way to sudden, frightening outbursts. His psychotic was not without a creepy, camp charm and he played his telephone conversations with Horrigan for malevolent black comedy, seeing them as an act of gamesmanship, a battle of wits between equals, flirting, taunting and humiliating him in front of his colleagues. Leary knew everything about the man: his private life, his drink problem, his divorce, his pain, his guilt. The telephone calls were among the screenplay's best moments.

Leary was a chilling murderer, dispatching two women bank clerks and then two men who were out fishing without a thought. He turned

Clint Eastwood in
In the Line of Fire

The assassination attempt at a fund-raising dinner was sharply edited, cutting from the bodyguards bundling the President out of the building through the kitchens to Leary taking Horrigan hostage. The film ended with a melodramatic duel in a hotel's glass lift and Leary's all too expected fall to his death.

Horrigan flirted with a Secret Service agent (a very cool Rene Russo) three decades his junior. Their barbed dialogue was very much in a wisecracking tradition which stretched back to the gangster movies of the 1940s and 1930s. The best joke was a visual one, when they were approaching a bed and the camera stayed at floor level, observing what they were discarding: not just clothes, but handcuffs, guns and blackjacks.

Rene Russo and Clint Eastwood in *In the Line of Fire*

out to be a disillusioned CIA assassin. He and Horrigan were two halves of the same person, mutually dependent, both feeling that the United States had once been very special and neither believing in her any more. Malkovich's quietly dangerous performance was an excellent foil for Eastwood.

Horrigan, tough yet vulnerable, was the prototype (so he said) of the heterosexual, white, over-50 American male. The assassin, by implication, was homosexual. There was an exciting chase on the rooftops which ended with Horrigan dangling over the edge, hanging on to Leary's hand. It was a scene which paid direct homage to Alfred Hitchcock's *Vertigo*, though Hitchcock would not have gone so far as to have his villain perform mock fellatio on the hero's revolver, daring him to shoot his load in his mouth and kill them both.

Eastwood is an actor who has always given more than you might suspect he's capable of, and here he does a little reprise of his *Unforgiven* portrait that is wonderfully strong on the kind of detail that doesn't draw attention to itself but makes or breaks a leading part.

Derek Malcolm, *Guardian*

What makes Eastwood so powerful in the part is the way he imbues the action of the present with the presence of the past . . . no other American star has a comparable artillery that he brings to bear. Eastwood knows his own limitations as an actor: he cannot become somebody else; he has to play an aspect of himself.

Iain Johnstone, *Sunday Times*

The two greatest landscapes in American cinema are Monument Valley and Clint Eastwood's face.

Nigel Andrews, *Financial Times*

A PERFECT WORLD

Directed by Clint Eastwood   1993

Butch Haynes, a hardened criminal serving 40 years for armed robbery, escaped from prison, taking Phillip Perry, a seven-year-old boy, hostage. The escaping convict was pursued by a Texan Ranger travelling in a high-tech mobile trailer. The story was set in 1963, two weeks before President Kennedy's fatal visit to Dallas. There were, in fact, two separate stories: the hunted, who was in total control of the situation, and the hunter, who was not. The action was absorbing so long as it stuck with the convict and the boy on the long, lonesome roads of rural Texas.

Kevin Costner, cast against type, was basic-ally too nice to be convincing as a hardened criminal. The little boy was never in any danger. Obsessed with his own childhood, Butch identified with Phillip and became his surrogate father. 'The best thing a man can hope to be,' he said, 'is a fine family man.' He was more paternal than criminal; yet he was capable of brutality and had killed two men. The first had killed his mum; the second was his fellow fugitive, who had molested Phillip.

Butch was an implacable enemy of child abusers. The most electrifying, the most frightening scene in the whole film was when he threatened a black farmer (Wayne Dehart, excellent), forcing him at gunpoint to say he loved his child. The change in his character was so sharp as to be unbelievable and was there only so that Phillip could have a dramatic reason to shoot and wound him. His death, a sentimental, tear-jerking, elegiac finale, took place in a lovely meadow. The film had opened with the same lyrical shot, when it had seemed to be a picture of a man asleep in the windswept grass.

Butch, the lifelong loser ('I ain't a good man. I ain't the worst neither, just a breed apart') was a role Clint Eastwood might have played when he was younger. Costner acted with intelli-gence, charm and dry humour; the performance could have done with more anger, more nihilism.

Eastwood was cast as Red Garnett, the Texan Ranger, a role so perfunctory there was not much he could do with it. Garnett had been the

Clint Eastwood in
A Perfect World

Clint Eastwood in
A Perfect World

arresting officer who had recommended that
the teenage Butch should be sent to prison. He
had hoped he would reform once he was away
from the home influence; instead prison had
turned him into an hardened criminal, just like
his dad.

Eastwood acted with rugged authority, but
the scenes in the mobile were never interesting
enough and the attempts to introduce some
sparring between him and an accompanying
criminologist (Laura Dern) didn't work as well
as the scenes between him and Rene Russo had

done in *In the Line of Fire*. The criminologist,
a feminist, merely came across as an
anachronism in 1963. There was also a feeble
attempt to introduce some comedy when the
governor's prize mobile became separated from
its driver and they all ended up in the trees.

Eight-year-old T. J. Crowther played the
hostage: a shy, sad little boy from a broken
home, denied the simplest pleasures because
his mother was a Jehovah's Witness. Phillip
looked cute in his Hallowe'en mask and got on
just fine with Butch, especially after Butch had

inflated by the presence of its two famous stars. The film should have been shorter, sharper, tougher, smaller; at 138 minutes, it was overlong and the pace was far too leisurely. There was too much narrative and not nearly enough suspense.

Eastwood is canny enough to hold on to at least one basic rule of American movies: if you get a big star and put him in a big landscape – Texas will do – you can't go far wrong.

Terence Rafferty, *New Yorker*

His tough-cop role resembles many others he's played before, but this time remains a strictly one-dimensional supporting figure who doesn't really do much.

Todd McCarthy, *Variety*

As the decent, grizzled Ranger, the self-abnegatory Eastwood never uses his power as director to upstage other actors.

Philip French, *Observer*

***A Perfect World* evinces the perfect integrity, the unstinting modesty of Eastwood's work all along. (The reticent directorial style meshes absolutely with the persona.)**

Georgina Brown, *Village Voice*

Its tone is pretty much unique, but then why would anyone set out to make a film that is sentimental without being sweet, that manages to be bleak and mawkish at the same time? The film is a mustard sandwich on white bread, bland in texture but still leaving a harsh taste in the mouth.

Adam Mars-Jones, *Independent*

reassured him about the size of his penis. ('It's a good size for a boy of your age.') The bonding of man and child was all the more touching for being saccharine-free. Crowther had been extremely well-directed and edited.

Bradley Whitford was cast as the odious, arrogant sharp-shooter who finished off the wounded Butch and was rewarded for his too eager marksmanship with a sock to the jaw by the Texan Ranger and a kick in the balls by the criminologist.

A Perfect World was a small-scale movie,

Chronology

FILM

DATE	TITLE	ROLE	SCREENPLAY	DIRECTOR
1955	Revenge of the Creature	Lab assistant	Martin Berkeley	Jack Arnold
1955	Tarantula	Pilot	Robert M. Fresco and Martin Berkeley	Jack Arnold
1955	Lady Godiva of Coventry	First Saxon	Oscar Brodney and Harry Ruskin	Arthur Lubin
1955	Francis in the Navy	Jonesby	Devery Freeman, based on the character Francis created by David Stern	Arthur Lubin
1955	Never Say Goodbye	Will	Charles Hoffman	Jerry Hopper
1956	The First Traveling Saleslady	Jack Rice	Devery Freeman and Stephen Longstreet	Arthur Lubin
1956	Star in the Dust	Ranch Hand	Oscar Brodney, based on the novel *Lawman* by Lee Leighton	Charles Haas
1957	Escapade in Japan	Pilot	Winston Miller	Arthur Lubin
1957	Lafayette Escadrille (a.k.a. Hell Bent for Glory)	George Moseley	A. S. Fleischman, from a story by William A. Wellman	William A. Wellman
1957	Ambush at Cimarron Pass	Keith Williams	Richard G. Taylor and John K. Butler. Story by Paul Sawtell and Bert Shefter	Jodie Copelan
1959–66	Rawhide (television series)	Rowdy Yates	various	various
1964	Per un pugno di dollari (English title: A Fistful of Dollars)	Joe	no acknowledgement on screen	Sergio Leone
1965	Per qualche dollari in più (English title: For a Few Dollars More)	Manco	Luciano Vincenzoni	Sergio Leone
1966	Il buono, il brutto, il cattivo (English title: The Good, the Bad and the Ugly)	Blondy	Age-Scarpelli, Luciano Vincenzoni and Sergio Leone	Sergio Leone
1966	Le Streghe (English title: The Witches)	Mario	Cesare Zavattini, Fabio Carpi and Enzo Muzii	Vittorio de Sica
1968	Hang 'Em High	Jed Cooper	Leonard Freeman and Mel Goldberg	Ted Post
1968	Coogan's Bluff	Coogan	Herman Miller, Dean Reisner and Howard Rodman. Story by Herman Miller	Don Siegel
1968	Where Eagles Dare	Schaffer	Alistair MacLean	Brian G. Hutton
1969	Paint Your Wagon	'Pardner'	screenplay and lyrics: Alan Jay Lerner; adaptation: Paddy Chayefsky; music: Frederick Loewe; music for additional songs: André Previn	Joshua Logan
1969	Two Mules for Sister Sara	Hogan	Albert Maltz. Story by Budd Boetticher	Don Siegel
1970	Kelly's Heroes	Kelly	Troy Kennedy Martin	Brian G. Hutton
1970	The Beguiled	John McBurney	John B. Sherry and Grimes Grice, from the novel by Thomas Cullinan	Don Siegel
1971	Play Misty for Me	Dave	Jo Heims and Dean Reisner. Story by Jo Heims	Clint Eastwood
1971	Dirty Harry	Harry Callahan	Harry Julian Fink and R. M. Fink and Dean Reisner. Story by Harry Julian Fink and R. M. Fink	Don Siegel
1972	Joe Kidd	Joe Kidd	Elmore Leonard	John Sturges
1972	High Plains Drifter	The Stranger	Ernest Tidyman	Clint Eastwood
1973	Breezy*	–	Jo Heims	Clint Eastwood
1973	Magnum Force	Harry Callahan	John Milius and Michael Cimino. Story by John Milius, based on characters created by Harry Julian Fink and R. M. Fink	Ted Post
1974	Thunderbolt and Lightfoot	Thunderbolt	Michael Cimino	Michael Cimino

DATE	TITLE	ROLE	SCREENPLAY	DIRECTOR
1975	The Eiger Sanction	Jonathan Hemlock	Hal Dresner, Warren B. Murphy and Rod Whitaker, based on the novel by Trevanian	Clint Eastwood
1976	The Outlaw Josey Wales	Josey Wales	Phil Kaufman and Sonia Chernus, from the novel *Gone to Texas* by Forrest Carter	Clint Eastwood
1976	The Enforcer	Harry Callahan	Stirling Silliphant and Dean Reisner. Story by Gail Morgan Hickman and S. W. Schurr, based on characters created by Harry Julian Fink and R. M. Fink	James Fargo
1977	The Gauntlet	Ben Shockley	Michael Butler and Dennis Shryack	Clint Eastwood
1978	Every Which Way But Loose	Philo Beddoe	Jeremy Joe Kronsberg	James Fargo
1979	Escape from Alcatraz	Frank Morris	Richard Tuggle, based on the book by J. Campbell Bruce	Don Siegel
1980	Bronco Billy	Billy McCoy	Dennis Hackin	Clint Eastwood
1980	Any Which Way You Can	Philo Beddoe	Stanford Sherman, based on characters created by Jeremy Joe Kronsberg	Buddy Van Horn
1982	Honkytonk Man*	Red Stovall	Clancy Carlile, based on his novel	Clint Eastwood
1982	Firefox*	Mitchell Gant	Alex Lasker and Wendell Wellmann, based on the novel by Craig Thomas	Clint Eastwood
1983	Sudden Impact*	Harry Callahan	Joseph C. Stinson. Story by Earl E. Smith and Charles. B. Pierce, based on characters created by Harry Julian Fink and R. M. Fink	Clint Eastwood
1984	Tightrope*	Wes Block	Richard Tuggle	Richard Tuggle
1984	City Heat	Lieutenant Speer	Sam O. Brown and Joseph C. Stinson from a story by Sam O. Brown	Richard Benjamin
1985	Pale Rider*	Preacher	Michael Butler and Dennis Shryack	Clint Eastwood
1986	Heartbreak Ridge*	Sergeant Tom Highway	James Carabatsos	Clint Eastwood
1986	Round Midnight**	–	Bertrand Tavernier	Bertrand Tavernier
1986	Ratboy**	–	Rob Thompson	Sondra Locke
1988	Bird*	–	Joel Oliansky	Clint Eastwood
1988	The Dead Pool	Harry Callahan	Steve Sharon. Story by Steve Sharon, Durk Pearson and Sandy Shaw, based on characters by Harry Julian Fink and R. M. Fink	Buddy Van Horn
1988	Thelonious Monk: Straight No Chaser**	–	documentary	Charlotte Zwerin
1989	Pink Cadillac	Tommy Nowak	John Eskow	Buddy Van Horn
1990	White Hunter, Black Heart*	John Wilson	Peter Viertel, James Bridges and Burt Kennedy, based on the novel by Peter Viertel	Clint Eastwood
1990	The Rookie	Nick Pulovski	Boaz Yakin and Scott Spiegel	Clint Eastwood
1992	Unforgiven*	William Munny	David Webb Peoples	Clint Eastwood
1993	In the Line of Fire	Frank Horrigan	Jeff Maguire	Wolfang Petersen
1993	The Man from Malpaso	Himself	documentary	Gene Feldman
1993	A Perfect World	Red Garnett	John Lee Hancock	Clint Eastwood
1995	The Bridges of Madison County	James Kincaid	Richard La Graveuse and Ronald Bass, from the novel by Robert James Waller	Clint Eastwood

* Clint Eastwood also producer. He did not appear in *Breezy* and *Bird*.
** Clint Eastwood producer only.

TELEVISION

1956	Highway Patrol	Syndicated
1956	TV Reader's Digest	
	episode: Cochise, Greatest of the Apaches	ABC
1957	Men of Annapolis	Syndicated
1957	Wagon Train *episode:* The Charles Avery Story	NBC
1958	Navy Log *episode:* The Lonely Watch	ABC
1958	West Point *episode:* White Fury	ABC
1959	Maverick *episode:* Duel at Sundown	ABC
1959–66	Rawhide	CBS
1962	Mr Ed *episode:* Clint Eastwood meets Mr Ed	CBS
1985	Vanessa in the Garden (director only)	NBC

Acknowledgements

The author would like to begin by thanking Barry Holmes, his editor.

The author and publishers express their appreciation to the Kobal Collection and the following companies for their assistance and/or permission in relation to the following photographs:

The Kobal Collection, frontispiece, pp. 6, 9, 10, 18, 20, 24, 25, 26, 29, 30–1, 32–3, 34, 35, 38–9, 40–1, 42–3, 45, 46, 47, 48–9, 51, 52, 53, 56, 57, 58, 59, 60–1, 62, 66, 70–1, 72, 73, 74, 75, 76–7, 79, 82, 83, 84–5, 87, 89, 92, 94, 95, 96, 97, 98, 100, 101, 102–3, 107, 108, 109, 111, 112–13, 114, 115, 116, 117, 118, 120–1, 122, 124, 130, 131, 132, 133, 134–5, 136, 140, 141, 142, 145, 146, 147, 149, 150–1, 152, 153, 154–5, 156, 157, 163, 164, 170, 171, 173, 174, 175, 178, 179, 180–1, 182, 184, 185; BFI Stills, Posters and Designs, pp. 12, 15, 21, 22–3, 81, 138–9, 143, 165; Columbia Tristar, pp. 182, 184; Columbia Warners, pp. 92, 94, 111; MGM, pp. 51, 52, 53, 65, 66, 67; Paramount Pictures, pp. 56, 62, 118, 120–1, 122; Technicolour, pp. 54–5; United Artists, pp. 45, 46, 95, 96, 97; Universal Pictures, pp. 2, 9, 20, 26, 47, 48–9, 50, 57, 58, 59, 60–1, 70–1, 72, 73, 74, 75, 83, 84, 85, 87, 89, 98, 100; Warner Bros, pp. 10, 76–7, 79, 101, 102–3, 104, 105, 108, 109, 115, 116, 124, 126–7, 130, 131, 132, 133, 134–5, 136, 137, 140, 147, 149, 150–1, 152, 153, 154–5, 158–9, 160, 163, 166, 169, 170, 171, 173, 174, 175, 176–7, 178, 179, 180–1, 185, 186–7; Warner Bros/Malpaso, pp. 141, 142, 145, 146, 156, 157, 162, 164, 166, 169.

The author would like to add a personal note of thanks to Christine Lloyd Lyons and her staff at the Kobal Collection and to everybody at the BFI reference library and stills department.

Awards and Honours

1971
Appointed by President Richard Nixon to the
    National Council of Arts

1980
New York Museum of Modern Art
    Retrospective of his films

1985
Cinémathèque Française
    Retrospective of his films
Chevalier des Arts et Lettres

1986–8
Mayor of Carmel, California

1987
Golden Globe
    Cecil B. de Mille Prize

1988
Golden Globe
    Best Director: *Bird*

1992
Los Angeles Film Critics Association
    Best Director: *Unforgiven*

The American Academy of Motion Picture Arts
and Sciences
    Best Director: *Unforgiven*
    Nomination for Best Actor: *Unforgiven*

Golden Globe
    Best Director: *Unforgiven*

1993
British Film Institute Fellowship
    NATO/Showest Director of the Year

1994
President of Cannes Film Festival Jury